WORLD WAR I

WORLD WAR I

A Concise Military History of "The War to End All Wars" and The Road to the War

Adapted from

American Military History
Office of the Chief
of Military History
United States Army

Maurice Matloff
General Editor

DAVID McKAY COMPANY, INC.
New York

Adapted from *American Military History*
Office of the Chief of Military History
United States Army

Maurice Matloff, General Editor

Contributing Editors:
Vincent C. Jones
Charles B. MacDonald
Maps by Maj. James P. Holly

Published by
David McKay Company, Inc.
2 Park Avenue
New York, N.Y. 10016

Library of Congress Cataloging in Publication Data

Main entry under title:

World War I.
Includes index.
1. European War, 1914-1918—United States.
2. European War, 1914-1918—Causes. 3. United States—
History—War of 1898.   I. Matloff, Maurice, 1915-
American military history.   II. United States. Dept. of
the Army. Office of Military History.
D570.W6   940.4'0973   79-9549
ISBN 0-679-51450-3

1 2 3 4 5 6 7 8 9 10

MANUFACTURED IN THE UNITED STATES OF AMERICA

CONTENTS

CHAPTER 1

Emergence to World Power 1898–1902

In the latter part of the nineteenth century the United States, hitherto largely provincial in thought and policies, began to emerge as a new world power. Beginning in the late 1880's more and more Americans displayed a willingness to support involvement of the nation in frankly imperialistic ventures, justifying this break with traditional policy on strategic, economic, religious, and emotional grounds. Much of the energy that had been channeled earlier into internal development of the country, and especially into westward expansion along the frontier (which, according to the Census Bureau, ceased to exist as of 1890), was now diverted to enterprises beyond the continental limits of the United States. It was only a matter of time before both the Army and the Navy were to be called upon to support and protect the new American interests overseas.

A New Manifest Destiny

This new manifest destiny first took the form of vigorous efforts to expand long-established American trade and naval

1

interests overseas, especially in the Pacific and Caribbean. Thus, in the Pacific the United States took steps to acquire control of coaling and maintenance stations for a growing steam-propelled fleet. In 1878 the United States obtained the right to develop a coaling station in Samoa and in 1889, to make this concession more secure, recognized independence of the islands in a tripartite pact with Great Britain and Germany. In 1893, when a new native government in Hawaii threatened to withdraw concessions, including a site for a naval station at Pearl Harbor, American residents tried unsuccessfully to secure annexation of the islands by the United States. Development of a more favorable climate of opinion in the United States in the closing years of the century opened the way for annexation of Hawaii in 1898 and Eastern Samoa (Tutuila) in 1899.

In the same period, the Navy endeavored with little success to secure coaling stations in the Caribbean, and Americans watched with interest abortive efforts of private firms to build an isthmian canal in Panama. American businessmen promoted establishment of better trade relations with Latin American countries, laying the groundwork for the future Pan American Union. And recurrent diplomatic crises, such as that with Chile in 1891-92, arising from a mob attack on American sailors in Valparaiso, and with Great Britain over the Venezuelan-British Guiana boundary in 1895, drew further attention to the southern continent.

Trouble in Cuba

While economic and strategic motives contributed significantly to the new manifest destiny, it was traditional American humanitarian concern for the oppressed peoples of Cuba that ultimately proved most important in launching the United States on an imperialistic course at the turn of the century. Cuba's geographic proximity to the United States and strategic location had long attracted the interest of American expansionists. Yet they were a small minority, and only when the Cubans rebelled against the repressive colonial policies of Spain did the attention of most Americans turn to the Caribbean island. This was true in 1868, when Cubans revolted against the Spanish regime in a rebellion destined to last for a decade, and again in 1895, when they rose up once more against continuing repression by the mother country. Many Americans soon favored some kind of intervention, but President Grover Cleveland was determined that the United States should adhere to a policy of strict neutrality. Events in Cuba, however, soon were to make this position increasingly difficult to maintain.

When after almost a year of costly fighting the Spanish had failed to suppress the rebellion, they turned to harsher measures. To carry these out the Madrid Government appointed a new Captain-General for Cuba, Valeriano Weyler, an officer with a reputation as an able soldier. Weyler arrived in Havana in early February 1896 with additional troops and immediately instituted new tactics designed to isolate the insurrectionist forces—entrenchments, barbedwire fences, and, at narrow parts of the island, lines of blockhouses. Simultaneously, he inaugurated a policy of *reconcentrado,* herding women, children, and old people from the countryside into detention camps and garrisoned towns, where thousands died from disease and starvation. Weyler's methods gave newspapers in the United States, especially those practicing a newly fashionable yellow journalism, opportunity for renewed attacks on Spanish policies in Cuba. They portrayed the Spanish general as an inhuman "butcher" inflicting his cruel tactics on high-minded patriots struggling bravely for freedom from the oppression of an out-dated Old World authoritarianism.

In early 1896 both houses of Congress adopted by overwhelming majorities concurrent resolutions proposing that the United States grant belligerent status to the insurgents and employ its good offices to gain Spain's recognition of Cuban independence. Politicians, both in and out of Congress, saw in the Cuban situation an opportunity to gain popular support in the upcoming election of 1896. And a few expansion-minded American leaders perceived the insurrection as a chance to acquire naval bases in the Caribbean and open the way further for the country to play a more prominent role in world affairs. But neither Cleveland, nor his successor as President in 1897, William McKinley, wanted a war with Spain.

The Republican party platform of 1896, however, committed McKinley to a policy of using the nation's "influences and good offices to restore peace and give independence . . ." to Cuba. Consistent with this pledge, the newly elected President, in the face of a crescendo of demands for immediate American intervention, worked courageously and patiently, seeking to find a diplomatic solution that would satisfy the Cuban insurrectionists yet avoid a conflict between the United States and Spain.

In early February 1898, after serious rioting in Havana, the jingoistic New York *Journal* published a private letter written by Enrique Dupuy de Lôme, the Spanish Minister in Washington, to a Spanish editor then traveling in the United States. This communication, which a Cuban official in the Havana Post Office had stolen and passed on to the newspaper, expressed de Lôme's adverse personal reaction to McKinley's message to Congress in December 1897. The President was, he thought, "weak and a bidder for admiration of the crowd . . . a would-be politician who tries to leave a door open behind himself while keeping on good terms with the jingoes in his party." For the majority of Americans this unprecedented insult to a President was only further confirmation of the arrogance and insolence with which they felt Spain regularly conducted its Cuban policies. Even de Lôme's prompt resignation did little to calm the storm of indignation that swept the country. Nevertheless when Spain, at American insistence, somewhat reluctantly offered an apology, McKinley was inclined to accept it. Privately he was horrified at the possibility that what he viewed as a strictly personal matter might lead to war.

Despite this development McKinley still might have achieved a diplomatic solution had the American battleship *Maine* not been sunk on February 15, 1898, in Havana harbor as a result of a mysterious explosion, with a loss of 260 lives. The vessel was in the port ostensibly on a courtesy

4

call—but actually to provide closer protection for American citizens in Cuba—dispatched there rather reluctantly by McKinley upon the advice of the American consul in Havana. A naval investigating commission appointed by the President announced on March 25 that the *Maine* had gone down as a result of an external explosion, which to most Americans indicated Spanish treachery. But McKinley, in reporting to Congress on the commission's verdict, once again counseled "deliberate consideration" and, on March 27, sent to Madrid a new plan for peaceful settlement of the Cuban problem. The Spanish reply on March 31 agreed to end the *reconcentrado* policy and arbitrate the *Maine* disaster, but procrastinated on granting the insurrectionists an immediate armistice and refused to accept mediation by McKinley or to promise eventual independence for Cuba.

In spite of this discouraging response from Spain, the President continued to move slowly, leaving the door open for last-minute negotiations. Twice he postponed his war message to Congress before finally delivering it on April 11. Eight days later Congress passed a joint resolution proclaiming Cuba independent and authorizing the President to take necessary measures to expel the Spanish from the island. It included a significant amendment by Senator Teller of Colorado forbidding annexation of Cuba. With this authorization McKinley immediately ordered a blockade of Cuba, and an American naval squadron promptly took up a position off Havana. On April 25 Congress declared a state of war had existed since April 21. So began the conflict with Spain which McKinley and Cleveland had tried so hard to avoid—a war for which, despite the months of negotiation preceding its outbreak, the country was militarily most ill prepared.

Mobilizing for War

The extent of unpreparedness for overseas combat varied considerably in the two military services. In the decade preceding the war, the Navy, thanks to the efforts of career officers such as Rear Adm. Stephen B. Luce and Capt. Alfred T. Mahan, and to Benjamin Tracy, Secretary of the Navy in Harrison's administration, and also to the willingness of Congress, in a period of expanding overseas interests and relative prosperity, to appropriate the necessary funds, had carried out an extensive construction and modernization program. During the same period, the Naval War College at Newport, Rhode Island (established in 1885 through the efforts of Admiral Luce), had provided the Navy with a strong corps of professional officers trained in the higher levels of warfare and strategy, including the far-ranging doctrines of Mahan.

The Army was not so fortunate. With an average size in the quarter of a century preceding 1898 of only about 26,000 officers and men, most of whom were scattered widely across the country in company- and battalion-size organizations, the Army never had an opportunity for training and experience in the operation of units larger than a regiment. And while the individual soldier was well trained, the Army lacked a mobilization plan, a well-knit higher staff, and experience in carrying on joint operations with the Navy. The National Guard, with somewhat more than 100,000 members, was composed mostly of infantry units. Still lacking a consistent program of supervision by the Regular forces, most Guard units were poorly trained and disciplined, understrength, and inadequately equipped. Thus, typically, although most Regulars by 1898 were armed with Krag-Jörgensen rifles firing smokeless powder cartridges, most Guardsmen were still equipped with Springfield rifles which could fire only black powder ammunition.

Despite obvious deficiencies, the Guard might have supplied many of the units used in the conflict had it not been for other factors that made it difficult to employ Guardsmen on short notice in overseas theaters of war. Under existing law, there was some question as to whether it was legal for Guard units to serve abroad. Furthermore, Guard organization varied greatly from state to state, and most Guardsmen objected to any move that would place them under control of the Regular Army for the sake of achieving greater

6

uniformity in organization. The War Department proposed to form a new federal volunteer force with officers appointed by the President. But again the Guard opposed this, and Congress in the mobilization act of April 22, 1898, settled for a makeshift arrangement providing for a wartime force composed of both Regular and volunteer units organized into brigades, divisions, and army corps. Some Guard units did, in effect, serve under an arrangement whereby if enough members of a state unit volunteered for service, they were kept together to form a comparable federal volunteer unit.

Although the act of April 22 provided for 125,000 volunteers, popular demand soon led Congress to increase this number by 75,000 and authorize additional special volunteer forces, including 10,000 enlisted men "possessing immunity from diseases incident to tropical climates"—the so-called Immunes. Simultaneously it also authorized more than doubling the size of the Regular Army to nearly 65,000. By war's end in August 1898, the Regular forces numbered 59,000 and the volunteers, 216,000, a total of 275,000.

Mobilizing, equipping, and supplying these wartime forces placed a severe burden upon the War Department. With neither a military planning staff nor the funds necessary to plan for war in peacetime, the department inevitably was ill prepared for any kind of major mobilization or military operation. Further complicating matters was a basic disagreement within the department concerning the strategy to be followed and the way mobilization should be carried out.

To the extent the United States had a strategy for conduct of the war against Spain in the Caribbean, it consisted of maintaining a naval blockade of Cuba while native insurgent forces carried on a harassing campaign against Spanish troops on the island. Supporters of this policy—Captain Mahan was among its more articulate advocates—believed that it would lead eventually to surrender of the Spanish forces and the freeing of Cuba. No direct clash between American and Spanish troops was visualized; American land

7

forces would simply occupy Cuba as soon as the Spanish departed.

More or less in conformity with this strategy, Maj. Gen. Nelson Miles, Commanding General of the Army, proposed to assemble, train, and equip a small force of about 80,000, using the Regular Army as a nucleus. There would be ample time for mobilizing this force, since Miles deemed it unwise to land any troops in Cuba before the end of the unhealthy rainy season in October. The first step was to concentrate the entire Regular Army at Chickamauga Park, Georgia, where it could receive much-needed instruction in combined arms operations.

So deliberate and cautious a plan, however, was, by mid-April 1898, not in harmony with the increasing public demand for immediate action against the Spanish. With an ear to this demand, Secretary of War Russell M. Alger, who had been a general officer in the Civil War and subsequently had pursued a political career for thirty years, ignored the advice of General Miles. He ordered the Regular infantry regiments to go to New Orleans, Tampa, and Mobile, where presumably they would be ready for an immediate descent on Cuba. *(Map 1)* (Later some infantry troops did go to Chickamauga Park, where they trained with the Regular cavalry and artillery concentrated there.)

The decision to mobilize large volunteer forces compounded the problems of equipping, training, and supplying the wartime Army. In the spring and summer of 1898, thousands of enthusiastic volunteers, a few with some militia training but most only raw recruits, poured into newly established camps in the South—located there so as to be near Cuba and, at the same time, help the soldiers to become accustomed to semitropical climatic conditions. But a taste of military life in the training camps soon curbed the enthusiasm of most volunteers, for there they found chronic shortages of the most essential equipment—even of such basic items as underwear, socks, and shoes—a steady diet of badly prepared food, unbelievably poor sanitary conditions, inadequate medical facilities, and a lack of up-to date weapons. Red tape and poor management in the War

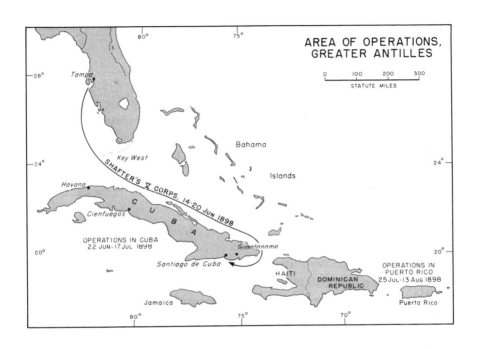

AREA OF OPERATIONS,
GREATER ANTILLES

0   100   200   300
STATUTE MILES

28°

Tampa

80°   75°

24°   24°

Key West   Bahama

Islands

Havana

Cienfuegos   C U B A

OPERATIONS IN CUBA
22 JUN-17 JUL 1898   Guantanamo

20°   20°

Santiago de Cuba   HAITI   DOMINICAN   OPERATIONS IN
REPUBLIC   PUERTO RICO
25 JUL-13 Aug 1898

Jamaica   Puerto Rico

80°   75°   70°

SHAFTER'S V CORPS, 14-20 JUN 1898

Department's supply bureaus (the Ordnance Department possibly excepted) continued to delay correction of some of the worst deficiencies and combined with the shortage of capable volunteer officers to limit the effectiveness and quality of training received in the camps.

A similar general inefficiency characterized the War Department's conduct of actual operations against Spain. Since Congress had provided no machinery in the department for peacetime co-ordination of foreign policy with the country's military posture, the nation went to war without any kind of over-all plan of operations or even adequate intelligence about the enemy or the Cuban insurgents. Suddenly confronted in April 1898 with the necessity for launching overseas amphibious attacks on hostile shores—under the best circumstances always a difficult type of operation, requiring careful planning and close interservice co-operation—the War Department bureaus and the Army high command found themselves almost totally unprepared. Given time, they might have devised at least adequate operational plans; but public opinion, political pressures, and the trend of events demanded the launching of an immediate expedition against the Spanish in Cuba.

Victory at Sea: Naval Operations in the Caribbean and Pacific

Fortunately, it turned out that the really decisive fighting of the war fell to the much better prepared Navy, although last-minute alterations in its strategic plan for dealing with the Spanish Fleet seriously threatened to reduce its effectiveness. Shortly after the war began, rumors circulated that an enemy fleet under Admiral Pascual Cervera y Topete was approaching the Atlantic coast of the United States. An alarmed public demanded that measures be taken to defend the Atlantic seaboard. In deference to this demand, the Navy Department in late April 1898 withheld some of its best fighting ships from Rear Adm. William T. Sampson's North Atlantic Squadron, sent to blockade Cuba. These ships, formed into a "flying squadron" under Commodore Winfield S. Schley, set up a watch for Cervera. This move was in conflict with the provisions in the Navy's strategical plan for a war with Spain. Based upon Mahan's doctrines, the plan called for maintaining Sampson's squadron at full strength in the Caribbean, ready to intercept any Spanish fleet sent out to relieve Cuba.

In the western Pacific, meantime, the Navy was able to adhere to its strategical plan—the latest version of which had been completed in June 1897. Worked out after 1895 by officers at the Naval War College in collaboration with the Office of Naval Intelligence, this plan, known to President McKinley and the high officials in the Navy Department, provided for an attack on the Philippines, leading to destruction of Spanish warships there, capture of Manila, and blockade of the principal Philippine ports. The basic objectives of the plan were to weaken Spain by cutting off revenues from the Philippines and to place the United States in the position of having something to offer the Spanish as an inducement to make peace after Cuba had been freed.

Active Navy preparation for war began in January 1898, and in late February Theodore Roosevelt, as Acting Secretary of the Navy (Secretary John D. Long was ailing), cabled orders to American naval commanders, instructing them to get their squadrons in readiness to carry out existing war plans against Spain. Commodore George Dewey of the Asiatic Squadron received instructions to assemble his ships at Hong Kong, where they could take on coal and supplies preparatory to an attack on the Philippines.

Thus, on April 24, when McKinley finally ordered the Asiatic Squadron to execute the war plan against the Philippines Dewey was ready. He sailed into Manila Bay on the night of April 30 and next morning located the Spanish warships at Cavite. In a few hours and without loss of a single American life, he sank or disabled the entire Spanish Fleet. In the days immediately following, he also silenced the land batteries defending Manila harbor, but the city itself continued to resist.

Since Dewey's 1,700 men were barely sufficient to maintain his own naval squadron, he requested dispatch of land forces from the United States to take Manila. In the two months before their arrival, he blockaded the port and gave assistance to Emilio Aguinaldo, Filipino insurgent leader, who, with Dewey's aid, had returned to the Philippines from exile in Hong Kong. Aguinaldo undertook guerrilla operations to keep the Spanish land forces in the vicinity of Manila. Dewey had to deal as well with the ticklish problem of British, French, and German naval contingents in Manila Bay, which arrived ostensibly to protect their nationals from the insurgents, but actually also to help uphold any claims their governments might advance to Filipino territory should the United States fail to take control over the islands. Most troublesome was the German squadron under Rear Adm. Otto von Diederichs, but Dewey's patience and firmness prevented a serious incident, and Berlin withdrew its fleet when it became apparent that the United States was not going to abandon the Philippines.

Operations in the Caribbean

As in the Pacific so also in the Caribbean the course of naval developments would determine when and where the Army undertook operations against Spanish land forces. During the early part of May 1898, the whereabouts of the Spanish Fleet under Admiral Cervera remained a mystery. Lacking this information, the Army could not fix precisely the point where it would launch an attack. Nevertheless, the War Department pushed preparations at Tampa, Florida, for an expedition under General Miles to be put ashore somewhere near Havana. But persistent rumors of the approach of the Spanish Fleet to Cuban waters delayed this expedition while the Navy searched further for Cervera. News at last reached Washington near the end of May that the Spanish admiral had skillfully evaded the American naval blockade and, on the 19th of the month, had slipped into the bay at Santiago de Cuba. *(See Map 1.)*

The Navy, at first not at all certain that it was actually

12

Cervera's fleet in Santiago, sent Admiral Sampson to inspect the harbor. As soon as the American naval commander had ascertained that the four cruisers and several smaller war vessels were indeed Spanish, he bombarded the forts at the entrance to Santiago Bay. Unable to silence them, Sampson decided against trying to run the heavily mined harbor entrance. Instead, he sent Lt. (jg) Richmond P. Hobson to bottle up the enemy fleet by sinking the collier *Merrimac* athwart the channel. When this bold project failed, Sampson requested land forces to seize the Spanish batteries, at the same time dispatching marines ashore to secure a site for a naval base east of Santiago. In the first land skirmish of the Cuban campaign, the marines quickly overcame enemy resistance and established the base at Guantánamo Bay.

Upon receipt of Sampson's request for land forces, the War Department, already under strong public pressure to get the Army into action, ordered Maj. Gen. William R. Shafter to embark with the V Corps from Tampa as soon as possible to conduct operations against Santiago in co-operation with the Navy. This corps was the only one of the eight that the War Department had organized for the war that was anywhere near ready to fight. Composed chiefly of Regular Army units, it had been assembling at Tampa for weeks when the order came on May 31 for its embarkation; it would require another two weeks to get the corps and its equipment on board and ready to sail for Cuba.

The slow pace of preparation and loading of the expedition was attributable to many factors. There was no over-all plan and no special staff to direct it. Although selected because of its port facilities and proximity to Cuba, Tampa, from the logistical point of view, proved to be a poor choice for marshaling a major military expedition. With only one pier for loading ships and a single-track railroad connecting with mainline routes from the north, the resulting backup of freight cars for miles delayed shipment of much needed supplies and equipment. Incoming soldiers waited interminably in uncomfortable railroad cars. When freight cars finally did reach the port area, there were no wagons to unload them and no bills of lading to indicate what was in them. When it came to loading the ships, of which there were not enough to carry the entire corps, supplies and equipment were put on board with little regard for unloading priorities in the combat zone should there be enemy resistance during the landings.

In spite of the confusion and inefficiency at Tampa, by June 14 nearly 17,000 men were ready to sail. On board were 18 Regular and 2 volunteer infantry regiments; 10 Regular and 2 volunteer cavalry squadrons, serving dismounted; 1 mounted cavalry squadron; 6 artillery batteries; and a machine gun (Gatling gun) company. The expedition comprised a major part of the Regular forces, including all of the Regular Negro combat regiments. Moving out from Tampa on the morning of the 14th, the V Corps joined its naval convoy next day off the Florida Keys and by June 20 had reached the vicinity of Santiago.

While the troops on board endured tropical heat, unsanitary conditions, and cold rations—the canned beef was especially unpalatable—Shafter and Sampson conferred on how to proceed against the Spanish in Santiago. Sampson wanted the Army to storm the fort on the east side of the bay entrance, driving the Spanish from their guns. Then his fleet could clear away the mines and enter Santiago Bay to fight Cervera's squadron. Lacking heavy artillery, Shafter was not sure his troops could take the fort, which crowned a steep hill. He decided instead to follow the suggestion of General Calixto Garcia, the local insurgent leader, and land his forces at Daiquirí, east of Santiago Bay. *(Map 2)*

On June 22, after heavy shelling of the landing areas, the V Corps began disembarking amid circumstances almost as confused and hectic as those at Tampa. Captains of many of the chartered merchant ships resisted bringing their vessels close inshore. Their reluctance slowed the landing of troops and equipment, already handicapped by a shortage of lighters (the Navy could not spare the additional ones needed). Horses, simply dropped overboard to get ashore on their own, swam out to sea in some instances and were lost. An alert enemy defense might well have taken advantage of the chaotic conditions to oppose the landings

Transports at Tampa.

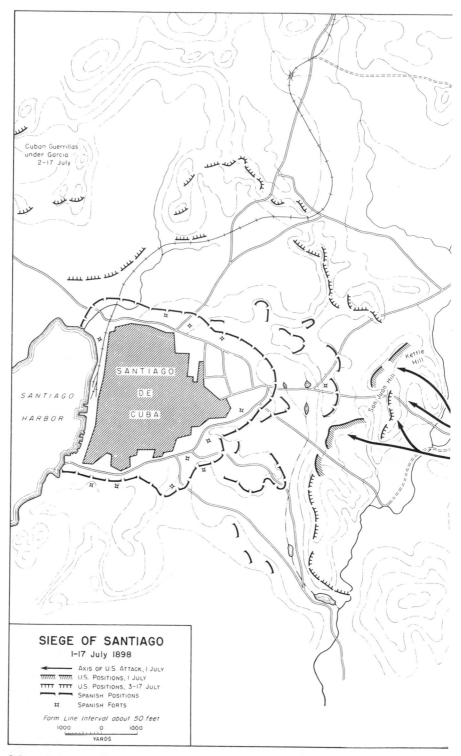

Cuban Guerrillas
under Garcia
2-17 July

SANTIAGO
DE
CUBA

SANTIAGO

HARBOR

San Juan Hill

Kettle
Hill

SIEGE OF SANTIAGO
1-17 July 1898

→ AXIS OF U.S. ATTACK, 1 JULY
⊥⊥⊥⊥ U.S. POSITIONS, 1 JULY
⊥⊥⊥⊥ U.S. POSITIONS, 3-17 JULY
⊥⊥⊥⊥ SPANISH POSITIONS
⊓ SPANISH FORTS

Form Line Interval about 50 feet
1000   0   1000
YARDS

MAP 2

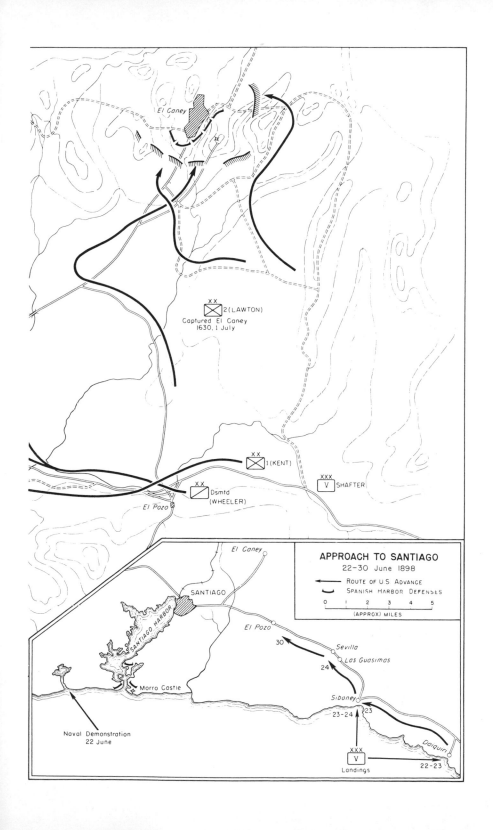

El Caney

XX
⊠ 2 (LAWTON)
Captured El Caney
1630, 1 July

XX
⊠ 1 (KENT)

XXX
V SHAFTER

XX
⊠ Dsmtd
(WHEELER)

El Pozo

El Caney

SANTIAGO

APPROACH TO SANTIAGO
22–30 June 1898

→ ROUTE OF U S ADVANCE
⌒ SPANISH HARBOR DEFENSES

0   1   2   3   4   5
(APPROX) MILES

SANTIAGO HARBOR

El Pozo

30

Sevilla
Las Guasimas

24

Morro Castle

Siboney

Naval Demonstration
22 June

23-24   23

XXX
V
Landings

22-23

Daiquiri

effectively. But the Spanish, though they had more than 200,000 troops in Cuba—some 36,000 of them in Santiago Province—did nothing to prevent Shafter's men from getting ashore. Some 6,000 landed on June 22 and most of the remaining 11,000 on the two days following. In addition, some 4,000 to 5,000 insurgents under General Garcia supplemented the American force.

The Battle of Santiago

Once ashore, elements of the V Corps moved westward toward the heights of San Juan, a series of ridge lines immediately east of Santiago, where well-entrenched enemy troops guarded the land approaches to the city. On June 23, Brig. Gen. Henry W. Lawton, commanding the vanguard, advanced along the coast from Daiquirí to occupy Siboney, which then became the main base of operations. The next day, Brig. Gen. Joseph Wheeler, the Confederate Army veteran, pushed inland along the road to Santiago with dismounted cavalry to seize Las Guásimas, after a brief skirmish with rear guard elements of a retiring Spanish force. This move brought American units within five miles of the San Juan Heights, where they paused for a few days while General Shafter assembled the rest of his divisions and brought up supplies. Even in this short time, Shafter could observe the debilitating effects of tropical climate and disease on his men. He was aware, too, that the hurricane season was approaching. Consequently, he decided in favor of an immediate attack on the defenses of Santiago.

Shafter's plan was simple: a frontal attack on the San Juan Heights. For this purpose, he deployed Brig. Gen. Jacob F. Kent's infantry division on the left and Wheeler's dismounted cavalry on the right, the entire force with supporting elements comprising some 8,000 troops. But before he made the main advance on the heights Lawton's infantry division with a supporting battery of artillery—more than 6,500 men—was to move some two miles north to seize the fortified village of El Caney, cutting off Santiago's water

18

supply and, if necessary, intercepting rumored Spanish reinforcements. This action completed—Shafter thought it would take about two hours—Lawton was to turn southwestward and form on the right flank of Wheeler's division for participation in the main assault. A brigade which had just landed at Siboney was to advance meanwhile along the coast in a feint to deceive the enemy.

The attack, which moved out at dawn on July 1, soon became badly disorganized because of poor co-ordination, difficult terrain, and tropical heat. The corpulent Shafter, virtually prostrated by the heat, had to leave the direction of the battle to others. At a stream crossing on the crowded main trail to San Juan Heights enemy gunners scored heavily when a towed Signal Corps balloon pinpointed the front of the advancing line of troops. And Lawton's division, delayed in its seizure of El Caney by a stubborn enemy defense, misplaced artillery, and the necessity of withdrawing a volunteer unit armed only with telltale black powder, did not rejoin the main force until after the assault had ended. Despite these unexpected setbacks, Kent's and Wheeler's divisions at midday launched a strong frontal attack on the Spanish forward defensive positions. Cavalry units of Wheeler's division, including the 9th Cavalry and part of the 10th, both Negro regiments, and the volunteer Rough Riders, who were commanded by Lt. Col. Theodore Roosevelt, seized Kettle Hill, separate from the central heights. Then Kent's infantry regiments, supported by the unorthodox employment of Gatling guns in the attack, stormed up San Juan Hill in the main ridge line, driving the Spanish from blockhouse and trench defenses and compelling them to retire to a strongly fortified inner line. Thus the day ended with the Americans having achieved most of their initial objectives. But the cost was high—nearly 1,700 casualties sustained since the start of operations against Santiago.

Concerned with the increasing sickness that was further thinning the ranks of the V Corps and faced by a well-organized Spanish second line of defense, General Shafter cabled Secretary Alger on July 3 that he was considering withdrawing about five miles to higher ground between the

THE SIGNAL CORPS BALLOON *at Santiago.*

San Juan River and Siboney. The shift would place his troops in a position where they would be less exposed to enemy fire and easier to supply. Alger replied that "the effect upon the country would be much better" if Shafter continued to hold his advanced position.

The V Corps commander then again sought to get the Navy to enter Santiago Bay and attack the city. But neither the Navy Department nor President McKinley was willing to sanction this move. Just when the whole matter threatened to become an embarrassing public debate between the two services, the Spanish themselves resolved the issue.

Deteriorating conditions within Santiago—lack of food and ammunition were seriously affecting the health and morale of the defending forces—convinced the defenders that the city must soon fall. While Cervera considered flight from the port hopeless, he had no recourse but to attempt it. Officials in both Havana and Madrid had ordered him, for reasons of honor, to escape when Santiago appeared about to surrender. Finally, on the morning of July 3, while Sampson and Shafter conferred ashore, Cervera made his dash for the open sea, hoping to reach the port of Cienfuegos on the south coast of Cuba. As soon as the Spanish Fleet appeared, Sampson's squadron, temporarily under command of Commodore Schley, gave chase and in less than two hours destroyed Cervera's fleet; four cruisers were crippled and run ashore and one destroyer was beached and another sunk.

A few days later, General Shafter persuaded the Spanish leaders in Santiago that they had no choice except to surrender. On July 16 they signed the unconditional terms demanded by the McKinley administration, which provided for surrender of 11,500 troops in the city and some 12,000 others in the vicinity of Santiago. The formal surrender ceremony took place on the following day.

During preparations for the Santiago campaign, General Miles personally had been overseeing organization of a second expedition to seize Puerto Rico. On July 21 he sailed from Guantánamo with more than 3,000 troops. His original strategy was to land first at Cape Fajardo in the northeast part of the island, where he could establish a base of operations for a subsequent advance westward to the capital, San Juan. For reasons not entirely clear, but probably because of a desire not to have to co-operate with the Navy in the attack on San Juan, Miles, while still at sea, changed his plans and on July 25 landed forces first at Guánica on the southeastern coast. Meeting virtually no opposition, the Americans shortly occupied the port of Ponce. In early August, after arrival of more than 10,000 additional troops from ports in the United States, General Miles, using Ponce as a base of operations, launched a four-column drive toward San Juan. There was little bloodshed—casualties for the campaign totaled fewer than fifty—and, in fact, most Puerto Ricans welcomed the American troops. The campaign ended on August 13 when word reached the island that Spain had signed a peace protocol the previous day.

Back in Cuba, meanwhile, conditions for the Army were much less pleasant. Spread of malaria, typhoid, and yellow fever among Shafter's troops at Santiago threatened to have far deadlier consequences than had the actual fighting. Concern over this problem led to the drafting of a joint letter by a number of Shafter's senior officers, proposing immediate evacuation of the Army from Cuba. Addressed to the commanding general, this round robin letter unfortunately came to the attention of the press before it reached Shafter. Hence, Washington officials read it in the newspapers before learning of its content from the general himself. Naturally the whole episode, coming at the time when peace negotiations were beginning, caused a sensation. Although acutely embarrassing for the Army and General Shafter, the incident did have the salutary effect of hastening measures to evacuate thousands of troops to Montauk Point, Long Island, where the Army Medical Department already had taken steps to establish an isolated detention camp. Here those who had contracted tropical infections received the necessary treatment. And out of the Army's nearly disastrous experience with the debilitating effects of disease and climate in Cuba came the impetus for the Medical Corps' notable project to determine the causes of

22

yellow fever, inaugurating a long-term program of research and study into what henceforth would be a permanent concern of the Army—the maintenance of the health and effectiveness of American troops in a tropical environment.

The Fall of Manila

In another tropical setting halfway around the world from Cuba the final military episode of the war took place. During May and June 1898 Admiral Dewey, while awaiting the arrival in the Philippines of land forces from the United States, kept in contact with the insurgent leader, General Aguinaldo. The Filipino forces occupied lines on the land side of Manila, preventing the Spanish garrison from moving beyond the immediate outskirts of the city.

Although the Americans and the Philippine insurgents shared a common interest in bringing about the defeat of the Spanish, relations between them tended to deteriorate during the period of waiting. The most important reason was a fundamental difference in objectives. The goal of the insurgents, who controlled most areas outside the towns and cities on Luzon and the other important islands, was immediate independence for the Philippines. But after some hesitation the McKinley administration and more and more Americans were coming around to the view that the United States ought to retain the islands. Once Aguinaldo became aware of this he endeavored to counteract it by taking steps to establish a revolutionary government with himself as president. On August 6 he appealed to foreign governments to recognize the independence of the Philippines. Hence by late summer there was serious doubt as to just what might be expected from the increasingly hostile insurgent forces.

In the interim, the long-awaited ground forces needed to complete the campaign in the Philippines began arriving in the Manila area. By the end of July 1898, some 13,000 volunteer and 2,000 Regular troops, constituting the VIII Corps under Maj. Gen. Wesley Merritt, had reached the islands. These troops had embarked from west coast ports (chiefly San Francisco) with a minimum of the confusion and difficulty that had characterized the launching of the Cuban expedition. In spite of the long voyage across the Pacific, they were in good condition and ready to start operations against the Spanish as soon as enough troops could be moved into the vicinity of Manila.

By early August General Merritt had 11,000 troops of the VIII Corps in lines immediately to the rear of those occupied by the insurgents, ready to attack the city. Inside the Philippine capital and in fortified lines just beyond the city walls were about 10,000 to 15,000 Spanish troops. Although their leaders were fully aware of the relative hopelessness of the situation, efforts of Dewey and Merritt to secure a peaceful surrender failed because the Spanish Government in Madrid insisted that the garrison should make at least a token show of resistance.

On the morning of August 13 the VIII Corps launched an assault on Manila. As the tide receded, American units moved quickly to the beaches on the south side of the city and then, supported by concentrated fire from Dewey's ships, advanced through the insurgent lines. By prior arrangement, somewhat reluctantly agreed to by Aguinaldo, the insurgents were to retire as the Americans moved toward the Spanish entrenchments. But in carrying out this difficult maneuver, Americans and insurgents unintentionally become intermixed and some troops—presumably for the most part insurgents—began firing on the Spanish lines. Momentarily, this flare-up threatened to thwart the enemy's plan to offer only token resistance, but quick action by American officers brought the firing under control and the garrison surrendered. Operations at Manila cost the Americans a total of 17 killed and 105 wounded.

Formal surrender ceremonies came the following day— actually two days after the government in Madrid had signed a peace protocol ending hostilities. News of the protocol had not yet reached Manila because the cable Dewey cut when he first entered Manila Bay still had not been repaired.

After negotiations in Paris in the fall of 1898, the United

24

States and Spain signed a treaty on December 10 ending the war. By its terms Spain gave up sovereignty over Cuba, which became an independent state, ceded Puerto Rico and Guam to the United States, and accepted $20 million in payment for the Philippines. Thus fatefully did Americans commit the nation to a new role as a colonial power in the Far East, with momentous future consequences that few at the turn of the century could anticipate.

The Philippine Insurrection, 1899–1902

Signing of the Treaty of Paris brought only a brief pause in military operations for the Army in the Philippines. With defeat and departure of the Spanish, the Americans inherited the complex problems of governing a populous Far Eastern archipelago about which they still knew relatively little. Even with full co-operation of all the heterogeneous peoples of differing cultures living in the islands, the task would have been formidable. Leaders of the native nationalist movement were no more ready to accept American rule peacefully than Spanish.

In the period following the fall of Manila while peace negotiations were in progress an uneasy truce existed between the insurgents and the American occupation forces. Under leadership of Aguinaldo, the insurgents established a provisional republic with a capital at Malolos, northeast of Manila, and organized a congress which began preparing a constitution. After the United States in January 1899 officially proclaimed possession of the Philippines and its intention to extend political control over all the islands, the insurgent congress ratified the constitution, formally establishing a Filipino republic, and prepared to resist the Americans.

The circumstances surrounding the start of fighting on the night of February 4, 1899, are vague. An insurgent patrol apparently deliberately challenged without provocation an American guard post near Manila. Since the incident occurred on the eve of ratification of the Treaty of Paris by

25

the United States Senate, it is conceivable that the insurgents may have wished by this surprise move to inflict an embarrassing setback on the Americans before reinforcements could arrive in the Philippines, hoping thus to influence the vote on the treaty. Or it may simply have been a spontaneous outburst, stemming from Aguinaldo's known inability to exercise very tight discipline over his loosely organized army. Whatever the reason, the VIII Corps reacted promptly and decisively. Against an estimated 40,000 insurgents in the Manila area, Maj. Gen. Elwell S. Otis, who had replaced General Merritt, could commit only about 12,000 of his 21,000 troops, since the remainder were volunteers scheduled to go home for early demobilization. Nevertheless, in extensive operations around the Philippine capital in the several days immediately following the attack on the 4th, the VIII Corps drove back the insurgents at all points, inflicting some 3,000 casualties, and then, late in the month, thwarted what appeared to be the beginning of a widespread uprising in the city, potentially fraught with the most serious consequences.

Although the insurgents suffered a severe setback in these first major engagements of the Philippine Insurrection, they continued more or less organized resistance on a smaller scale for more than two years, with spasmodic outbursts in the Visayas, the islands immediately south of Luzon. The Americans also met resistance from the predominantly Moslem Moro peoples residing in Mindanao and the Sulu Archipelago in the southern Philippines, areas where even the Spanish during their long period of rule had never exercised effective control.

When news of the insurrection reached Washington it quickly dispelled any doubts the McKinley administration might have had concerning the need for more troops in the Philippines to establish effective American control. The War Department responded promptly, arranging to raise ten additional federal volunteer regiments and, at the same time, ordering immediate dispatch of much needed Regular units to the islands. By late summer of 1899, more than 35,000 additional troops had joined the VIII Corps and more were on the way. Before it ended more than 100,000 American soldiers took part in some phase of the Philippine Insurrection.

Short of firearms and ammunition, the insurgents depended primarily upon unconventional tactics. Avoiding open confrontation with the better armed and organized Americans whenever possible, they relied upon surprise attacks and ambush, where bolo knives and other more primitive weapons could be employed with the most devastating effect. Resort to guerrilla operations enabled the insurgents to exploit their superior knowledge of the jungle and the mountainous country in which much of the fighting took place. To cope with these tactics, the Army found itself drawing upon its long experience in fighting the western Indians. Hampered logistically by the lack of roads and by rough terrain in the interior, the Americans had to depend primarily upon small arms fire and the bayonet in repelling hit-and-run insurgent attacks. Keeping the poorly organized and poorly co-ordinated insurgent bands under constant pursuit and pressure, VIII Corps troops gradually extended their control over most of Luzon and the other important islands.

Beginning in April 1899, the Army carried out a series of carefully co-ordinated offensives, aimed at securing control of the important population centers and lines of communications as a first step in establishing stable government and restoring normal economic activities. Immediately after the outbreak of insurgent hostilities in February, American columns had pushed north, south, and east from Manila, capturing the rebel capital at Malolos, and securing the Pasig River, which cut the main line of communications between insurgent forces in north and south Luzon. Now in April, General Otis sent General Lawton, veteran of the Santiago campaign, south toward Santa Cruz in the Laguna de Bay area and Maj. Gen. Arthur MacArthur north up the central plain from Malolos toward San Fernando. By mid-May, the success of these drives had seriously undermined insurgent ability to continue organized resistance and forced Aguinaldo to flee to the mountains in northern Luzon.

Advent of the rainy season and shortage of manpower halted further operations until fall.

In the autumn of 1899, General Otis launched a three-pronged drive in north central Luzon against Aguinaldo's remaining forces. Moving up on the right, Lawton recaptured San Isidro and approached San Fabian on Lingayen Gulf; MacArthur, in the center, seized Tarlac and reached Dagupan; Brig. Gen. Loyd Wheaton, on the left, went by ship from Manila to San Fabian, moving inland to defeat the insurgents at San Jacinto, and then linked up with MacArthur at Dagupan. Aguinaldo again managed to escape, but eventually was captured in March 1901 through a ruse skillfully carried out by a small party of Filipino scouts and American soldiers led by Brig. Gen. Frederick Funston.

Operations in the winter of 1899-1900 cleared insurrectionist remnants from the Manila region and permanently secured important lines of communications in central Luzon. By March 1900 the Army also controlled southern Luzon and the Visayas. In May, Otis, believing the insurrection virtually over, requested his own relief and General MacArthur replaced him. Events proved Otis mistaken, for the Army had to continue in the field for many more months, dealing with sporadic but persistent resistance in numerous small engagements. The guerrilla warfare was bitter and costly, resulting in more casualties for the Army than in the entire preceding fifteen months of extensive military operations. In early 1902, unrest among the Moros in Mindanao and the Sulu Archipelago intensified, and was by no means really settled when President Theodore Roosevelt announced on July 4 the formal end of the Philippine Insurrection.

The Boxer Uprising

Acquisition of the Philippines tended to stimulate further a growing interest in China among Americans for both commercial and humanitarian reasons. One important argument advanced for retaining the Philippines was that they would serve as a convenient way station in carrying on trade and protecting American interests in the Manchu empire. The dominant problem in China at the end of the nineteenth century was its threatened partition by the Great Powers. Both the Americans and the British opposed this, and in September 1899 the United States announced it had secured agreement from the interested powers for maintenance of an Open Door policy in their relations with China.

The already extensive exploitation of their country by foreign states, however, had aroused widespread resentment among younger Chinese. They formed the nucleus of a secret group called Boxers by Westerners which, with tacit support of the Dowager Empress, undertook a campaign against foreign influences and foreigners. By early 1900 this movement had brought much of China to the verge of revolution. Boxers in the northern provinces attacked and killed hundreds of Chinese Christians and foreigners, mostly missionaries. The wave of violence was climaxed by murder of the German Minister on June 20. In fear for their lives in what appeared to be the beginning of a general uprising, most remaining foreigners as well as many Chinese converts fled to the foreign legations area in Peking, defended by a composite force of some 600 soldiers and civilians. Soon they were besieged there by a much larger force of Boxers assisted by Chinese imperial troops.

Although the McKinley administration disliked the idea of becoming involved in an election year in an international incident with overtones of entangling foreign alliances, it agreed to join with the other powers in taking such steps as seemed necessary to rescue their beleaguered nationals. In establishing the limits of American diplomatic co-operation with the intervening powers, Secretary of State John Hay admonished the United States Minister that ". . . we have no policy in China except to protect with energy American interests and especially American citizens. . . . There must be no alliances." And on July 3 Hay circulated a second Open Door note among the interested powers, stating that it was the policy of the United States "to seek a solution which may bring about permanent safety and peace to China, preserve Chinese territorial and administrative entity, protect all rights guaranteed to friendly powers by treaty and international law, and safeguard for the world the principle of equal and impartial trade with all parts of the Chinese Empire."

Already in June the Navy's China squadron, under Rear Adm. Louis Kempff, had joined with other foreign naval units in bombardment of the Taku forts guarding Tientsin, the port city nearest to Peking, and had supplied a contingent for an international landing force composed of marines and other available troops. Formed into a rescue column, including more than a hundred Americans, this force had encountered overwhelming opposition and failed to break through to Peking. The powers then had taken immediate steps to organize a large relief expedition to drive through to the Chinese capital.

Because of the Philippine Insurrection the United States had sizable Army units available fairly near China. It could therefore contribute one of the larger contingents to the international relief force. Although General MacArthur, commanding in the Philippines, was somewhat reluctant to weaken his already overextended forces, he agreed to dispatch to China immediately the 9th Infantry and later the 14th Infantry and some artillery units. Other units, including the 6th Cavalry, came directly from the United States. Using Manila as a base and Nagasaki, Japan, as an advance port, the United States eventually assembled some 2,500 soldiers and marines in China under command of Maj. Gen. Adna R. Chaffee. On July 13, elements of this force, officially designated the China Relief Expedition, participated with troops from several other nations in the attack on Tientsin, which surrendered on the same day.

By early August, an allied force of some 19,000, including British, French, Japanese, Russian, German, Austrian, Italian, and American troops, was ready to move out of Tientsin toward Peking, some seventy miles distant. Fighting a number of sharp skirmishes en route, this force reached the Manchu capital on August 12 and prepared immediately to assault the gates leading into the Outer City. Lacking effective central direction, the relief expedition's attack was poorly executed. The Russian contingent prematurely forced an entrance into the Outer City on August 13, only to be thrown into confusion and require rescue by other allied troops. The next day, in a more carefully co-ordinated assault, elements of the U.S. 14th Infantry scaled the so-called Tartar Wall and provided cover for the British as they entered the Outer City in force, relieving the legations compound. Then on August 15, Capt. Henry J. Reilly's Light Battery F of the U.S. 5th Artillery shattered the gates leading into the Inner City with several well-placed salvos, opening the way for the allied troops to occupy the center of Peking. Although American troops had suffered comparatively light losses—slightly more than 200 killed and wounded—they did not take part in subsequent military operations, which consisted primarily of suppressing scattered Boxer elements and rescuing foreigners in the provinces. The McKinley administration, anxious to avoid further involvement in China, wanted to get Army units back to the Philippines before winter.

In a few months all resistance had ended and the Dowager Empress sued for peace, offering to pay an indemnity and reaffirm previously existing commercial concessions. During prolonged negotiations an international army of occupation to which the United States contributed a small contingent of Regulars remained in north China. It was withdrawn in September 1901 under terms of the Boxer Protocol. This agreement also provided that the powers maintain a fortified legation in Peking, garrison the Tientsin-Peking railway—an American contingent served as a part of this force until 1938—and receive reparations of $333 million. Of this amount the United States claimed only $25 million. In a few years it became apparent that even this sum was more than was needed to indemnify claims of American nationals and in 1907, and again in 1924, the United States returned portions totaling nearly $17 million to China, which placed the money in a trust fund for education of Chinese youths in both countries.

Participation of the United States in the Boxer Uprising at

the beginning of the twentieth century marked the first time since the American Revolution that the country had joined with other powers in an allied military operation. The intervention in China represented one more instance of the gradual change taking place at the turn of the century in the traditional policies and attitudes of the United States in world affairs as a result of the triumph of imperialism. As they entered the new century most Americans still believed that despite the acquisition of overseas colonies the nation could continue to adhere to the historic principles of isolationism. Developments in the early years of the twentieth century would demonstrate, however, that the nation had to make changes and adjustments in many long-established institutions and policies—including those relating to military defense of the country—to meet the requirements of its new status as a world power.

CHAPTER 2

Transition and Change, 1902-1917

For the United States the opening years of the twentieth century were a time of transition and change. At home they marked the beginning of a peaceful revolution—often designated the "Progressive Era"—when political leaders such as Theodore Roosevelt undertook to solve the economic and social problems arising out of the rapid growth of large-scale industry in the late nineteenth century. Increasing public awareness of these problems as a result of the writings of the "Muckrakers" and social reformers provided popular support for efforts to solve them by legislative and administrative measures. In foreign affairs it was a period when the country had to begin adjusting its institutions and policies to the requirements of its new status as a world power. In spite of a tendency after the end of the War with Spain to follow traditional patterns and go back to essentially isolationist policies, the nation's new responsibility for overseas possessions, its expanding commercial interests abroad, and the continued unrest in the Caribbean made a reversion to insularity increasingly unfeasible.

The changing conditions at home and abroad inevitably affected the nation's military establishment. During the decade and a half between the War with Spain and American involvement in World War I, both the Army and the

Navy would undergo important reforms in organization and direction. Although the United States did not become a participant in any major conflict during these years, both services were frequently called upon to assist with administration of the newly acquired overseas possessions. Both aided with protection of investments abroad threatened by native insurrections, revolutions, and other internal disturbances. And both contributed in other ways to upholding the vital interests of the nation in an era of greatly increased competition for commercial advantage and colonial empire.

Modernizing the Armed Forces

The intensification of international rivalries led most of the Great Powers to seek additional protection and advantage in diplomatic alliances and alignments. By the early years of the twentieth century the increasingly complex network of agreements had resulted in a new and precarious balance of power in world affairs. This balance was constantly in danger of being upset, particularly because of an unprecedented arms race, characterized by rapid enlargement of armies and navies and development of far more deadly weapons and tactics. While the United States remained aloof from "entangling alliances," it nevertheless continued to modernize and strengthen its own armed forces, giving primary attention to the Navy—the first line of defense.

The Navy's highly successful performance in the Spanish-American War increased the willingness of Congress and the American public to support its program of expansion and modernization. For at least a decade after the war Theodore Roosevelt, Senator Henry Cabot Lodge of Massachusetts, and other leaders who favored a "Big Navy" policy with the goal of an American fleet second only to that of Great Britain experienced little difficulty in securing the necessary legislation and obtaining the funds required for the Navy's expansion program.

For the Navy another most important result of the War

with Spain was the decision to retain possessions in the Caribbean and the western Pacific. In the Caribbean the Navy acquired more bases for its operations such as that at Guantánamo Bay in Cuba. The value of these bases soon became apparent as the United States found itself intervening more frequently in the countries of that region to protect its expanding investments and trade. In the long run, however, acquisition of the Philippines and Guam was even more significant, for it committed the United States to defense of territory thousands of miles distant from the home base. American naval strength in the Pacific had to be increased immediately to insure maintenance of a secure line of communications for the land forces that had to be kept in the Philippines. One way to accomplish this increase, with an eye to economy of force, was to build a canal across the Isthmus of Panama, so that Navy ships could move more rapidly from the Atlantic to the Pacific as circumstances demanded. Another was to acquire more bases in the Pacific west of Hawaii, which was annexed in 1898. Japan's spectacular naval victories in the war with Russia and Roosevelt's dispatch of an American fleet on a round-the-world cruise lasting from December 1907 to February 1909 drew public attention to the problem. But most Americans failed to perceive the growing threat of Japan to United States possessions in the western Pacific, and the line of communications to the Philippines remained incomplete and highly vulnerable.

The Navy fared much better in its program to expand the fleet and incorporate the latest technological developments in ship design and weapons. The modernization program that had begun in the 1880's and had much to do with the Navy's effectiveness in the Spanish-American War continued in the early 1900's. Construction of new ships, stimulated by the war and Roosevelt's active support, continued at a rapid rate after 1898 until Taft's administration, and at a somewhat slower pace thereafter. By 1917 the United States had a Navy unmatched by any of the Great Powers except Great Britain and Germany.

The Army, aware of the serious deficiencies revealed in

the War with Spain and of the rapid technological changes taking place in the methods of warfare, also undertook to modernize its weapons and equipment. Development of high-velocity, low-trajectory, clip-loading rifles capable of delivering a high rate of sustained fire had already made obsolete the Krag-Jörgensen rifle, adopted by the Army in 1892. In 1903 the Regular Army began equipping its units with the improved bolt-action, magazine-type Springfield rifle, which incorporated the latest changes in weapons technology. The campaigns of 1898 also had shown that the standard rod bayonet was too flimsy; starting in 1905, the Army replaced it by a one pound knife bayonet with a 16-inch blade. In 1906 addition of a greater propellant charge in ammunition for the Springfield provided even higher muzzle velocity and deeper penetration of the bullet. Combat at close quarters against the fierce charges of the Moros in the Philippines demonstrated the need for a hand arm less cumbersome and having greater impact than the .38-caliber revolver. The Army found the answer in the recently developed .45-caliber Colt automatic pistol, adopted in 1911.

Far more significant in revolutionizing the nature of twentieth century warfare than these improved hand weapons was the rapid-firing machine gun. The manually operated machine gun—the Gatling gun—which the Army had adopted in 1866, was employed successfully in the Indian wars and the Spanish-American War. American inventors, including Hiram Maxim, John Browning, and Isaac N. Lewis, the last an officer in the Army's coast artillery, took a leading part in developing automatic machine guns in the years between the Civil War and World War I. Weapons based upon their designs were adopted by many of the armies of the world. But not until fighting began in World War I was it generally realized what an important role the machine gun was to have in modern tactics. Thus in the years between 1898 and 1916, Congress appropriated only an average of $150,000 annually for procurement of machine guns, barely enough to provide four weapons for each Regular regiment and a few for the National Guard. Finally

36

in 1916 Congress voted $12 million for machine gun procurement, but the War Department held up its expenditure until 1917 while a board tried to decide which type of weapon was best suited to the needs of the Army.

Development of American artillery and artillery ammunition continued to lag behind that of western European armies. The Army did adopt in 1902 a new basic field weapon, the 3-inch gun with an advanced recoil mechanism. Also, to replace the black powder that had been the subject of such widespread criticism in the War with Spain, both the Army and the Navy took steps to increase the domestic output of smokeless powder. By 1903 production was sufficient to supply most American artillery.

Experience gained in the Spanish-American War also brought some significant changes in the Army's coastal defense program. The hurriedly improvised measures taken during the war to protect Atlantic ports from possible attack by the Spanish Fleet emphasized the need for modern seacoast defenses. Under the strategical concepts in vogue, construction and manning of these defenses were primarily an Army responsibility since in wartime the naval fleet had to be kept intact, ready to seek out and destroy the enemy's fleet. On the basis of recommendations by the Endicott Board, the Army already had begun an ambitious coastal defense construction program in the early 1890's, and in 1905 a new board headed by Secretary of War William Howard Taft made important revisions in this program with the goal of incorporating the latest techniques and devices. Added to the coastal defense arsenal were fixed, floating, and mobile torpedoes and submarine mines. At the same time, the Army's Ordnance Department tested 16-inch rifles for installation in the coastal defense fortifications, in keeping with the trend toward larger and larger guns to meet the challenge of naval weapons of ever-increasing size.

Of the many new inventions that came into widespread use in the early twentieth century in response to the productive capacity of the new industrial age, none was to have greater influence on military strategy, tactics, and organization than the internal combustion engine. It made possible the motor vehicle, which, like the railroad in the previous century, brought a revolution in military transportation, and the airplane and tank, both of which would figure importantly in World War I.

Reorganization of the Army: Establishment of the General Staff

After the Spanish-American War the Army also underwent important organizational and administrative changes aimed in part at overcoming some of the more glaring defects revealed during the war. Although the nation had won the war with comparative ease, many Americans realized that the victory was attributable more to the incompetence of the enemy than to any special qualities displayed by the Army. In fact, as a postwar investigating commission appointed by President McKinley and headed by Maj. Gen. Granville M. Dodge brought out, there was serious need for reform in the administration and direction of the Army's high command and for elimination of widespread inefficiency in the operations of the War Department.

No one appreciated the need for reform more than Elihu Root, a New York lawyer appointed Secretary of War in 1899 by McKinley. The President had selected Root primarily because he seemed well qualified to solve the legal problems that would arise in the Army's administration of recently acquired overseas possessions. But Root quickly realized that if the Army was to be capable of carrying out its new responsibilities as an important part of the defense establishment of a world power, it had to undergo fundamental changes in organization, administration, and training. Root, as a former corporation lawyer, tended to see the Army's problems as similar to those faced by business executives. "The men who have combined various corporations . . . in what we call trusts," he told Congress, "have reduced the cost of production and have increased their efficiency by doing the very same thing we propose you shall do now, and it does seem a pity that the Government of the United States should be the only great industrial establishment that cannot profit by the lessons which the world of industry and of commerce has learned to such good effect."

Beginning in 1899, Root outlined in a series of masterful reports his proposals for fundamental reform of Army institutions and concepts to achieve that "efficiency" of organization and function required of armies in the modern world. He based his proposals partly upon recommendations made by his military advisers (among the most trusted were Maj. Gen. Henry C. Corbin, The Adjutant General, and Lt. Col. William H. Carter) and partly upon the views expressed by officers who had studied and written about the problem in the post-Civil War years. Root arranged for publication of Col. Emory Upton's *The Military Policy of the United States* (1904), an unfinished manuscript which advocated a strong, expansible Regular Army as the keystone of an effective military establishment. Concluding that after all the true object of any army must be "to provide for war," Root took prompt steps to reshape the American Army into an instrument of national power capable of coping with the requirements of modern warfare. This objective could be attained, he hoped, by integrating the bureaus of the War Department, the scattered elements of the Regular Army, and the militia and volunteers.

Root perceived as the chief weakness in the organization of the Army the long-standing division of authority, dating back to the early nineteenth century, between the Commanding General of the Army and the Secretary of War. The Commanding General exercised discipline and control over the troops in the field while the Secretary, through the military bureau chiefs, had responsibility for administration and fiscal matters. Root proposed to eliminate this division of authority between the Secretary of War and the Commanding General and to reduce the independence of the bureau chiefs. The solution, he suggested, was to replace the Commanding General of the Army with a Chief of Staff, who would be the responsible adviser and executive agent of the President through the Secretary of War. Under Root's proposal, formulation of broad American policies would continue under civilian control.

A lack of any long-range planning by the Army had been another obvious deficiency in the War with Spain, and Root proposed to overcome this by the creation of a new General Staff, a group of selected officers who would be free to devote full time to preparation of military plans. Planning in past national emergencies, he pointed out, nearly always had been inadequate because it had to be done hastily by officers already overburdened with other duties. Pending Congressional action on his proposals, Root in 1901 appointed an *ad hoc* War College Board to act as an embryonic General Staff. In early 1903, in spite of some die-hard opposition, Congress adopted the Secretary of War's recommendations for both a General Staff and a Chief of Staff, but rejected his request that certain of the bureaus be consolidated.

By this legislation Congress provided the essential framework for more efficient administration of the Army. Yet legislation could not change overnight the long-held traditions, habits, and views of most Army officers, or of some Congressmen and the American public. Secretary Root realized that effective operation of the new system would require an extended program of re-education. This need for re-education was one important reason for the establishment of the Army War College in November 1903. Its students, already experienced officers, would receive education in problems of the War Department and of high command in the field. As it turned out they actually devoted much of their time to war planning, becoming in effect the part of the General Staff which performed this function.

In the first years after its establishment the General Staff achieved relatively little in the way of genuine staff planning and policy making. While staff personnel did carry out such appropriate tasks as issuing in 1905 the first Field Service Regulations for government and organization of troops in the field, drawing up the plan for an expeditionary force sent to Cuba in 1906, and supervising the Army's expanding school system, far too much of their time was devoted to day-to-day routine administrative matters.

The General Staff did make some progress in overcoming its early weaknesses. Through experience, officers assigned to the staff gradually gained awareness of its real purpose and powers. In 1910 when Maj. Gen. Leonard Wood became Chief of Staff he reorganized the General Staff, eliminating many of its time-consuming procedures and directing more of its energies to planning. With the backing of Secretary of War Henry L. Stimson (1911-13), Wood dealt a decisive blow to that element in the Army itself that opposed the General Staff. In a notable controversy, he and Stimson forced the retirement in 1912 of the leader of this opposition, Maj. Gen. Fred C. Ainsworth, The Adjutant General.

The temporary closing of most Army schools during the Spanish-American War and the need to co-ordinate the Army's educational system with the Root proposals for creating a War College and General Staff had provided an opportunity for a general reorganization of the whole system, with the over-all objective of raising the standards of professional training of officers. In 1901 the War Department directed that the schools of instruction for officers thereafter should be the Military Academy at West Point; a school at each post of elementary instruction in theory and practice; the five service schools—the Artillery School, Engineer School of Application, School of Submarine Defense (mines and torpedoes), School of Application for Cavalry and Field Artillery, and Army Medical School; a General Staff and Service College at Leavenworth; and a War College. The purpose of the school at Leavenworth henceforth was to train officers in the employment of combined arms and prepare them for staff and command positions in large units. To meet the requirements for specialized training as a result of new developments in weapons and equipment, the Army expanded its service school system, adding the Signal School in 1905, the Field Artillery School in 1911, and the School of Musketry in 1913.

41

Creation of the General Staff unquestionably was the most important organizational reform in the Army during this period, but there were also a number of other changes in the branches and special staff designed to keep the Army abreast of new ideas and requirements. The Medical Department, for example, established Medical, Hospital, Army Nurse, Dental, and Medical Reserve Corps. In 1907 Congress approved of division of the artillery into the Coast Artillery Corps and the Field Artillery, and in 1912 it enacted legislation consolidating the Subsistence and Pay Departments with the Quartermaster to create the Quartermaster Corps, a reform earlier recommended by Secretary Root. The act of 1912 also established an enlisted Quartermaster service corps, marking the beginning of the practice of using service troops instead of civilians and combat soldier details.

In the new field of military aviation, the Army failed to keep pace with early twentieth century developments. Contributing to this delay were the reluctance of Congress to appropriate funds and resistance within the military bureaucracy to diversion of already limited resources to a method of warfare as yet unproved. The Army did not entirely neglect the new field—it had used balloons for observation in both the Civil and Spanish-American Wars and, beginning in 1898, the War Department subsidized for several years Samuel P. Langley's experiments with power-propelled, heavier-than-air flying machines. In 1908, after some hesitation, the War Department made funds available to the Aeronautical Division of the Signal Corps (established a year earlier) for the purchase and testing of Wilbur and Orville Wright's airplane. Although the Army accepted this airplane in 1909, another two years passed before Congress appropriated a relatively modest sum—$125,000—for aeronautical purposes. Between 1908 and 1913, it is estimated that the United States spent only $430,000 on military and naval aviation, whereas in the same period France and Germany each expended $22 million, Russia, $12 million, and Belgium, $2 million. Not until 1914 did Congress authorize establishment of a full-fledged Aviation Section in the Signal Corps. The few military airplanes available for service on the Mexican border in 1916 soon broke down, and the United States entered World War I far behind the other belligerents in aviation equipment, organization, and doctrine.

Reorganization of the Army: The Regular Army and the Militia

In the years after the Spanish-American War nearly a third of the Regular Army troops, on the average, served overseas. Most were in the Philippines suppressing the insurrection and when that conflict officially ended in mid-1902, stamping out scattered resistance and organizing and training a native force known as the Philippine Scouts. Other Regulars were garrisoned in Alaska, Hawaii, China, and elsewhere. To carry out its responsibilities abroad and to maintain an adequate defense at home, the Regular Army from 1902 to 1911 had an average of about 75,000 officers and men, far below the 100,000 that Congress had authorized in 1902 to fill thirty infantry and fifteen cavalry regiments, supported by a corps of artillery. To make up for this deficiency in size of the Regular forces and at the same time to remedy some of the defects revealed in the mobilization for the War with Spain, the planners in the War Department recommended a reorganization of the volunteer forces.

Secretary Root took the lead in presenting to Congress in 1901 a program for reform of the National Guard. In response to his recommendations, Congress in 1903 passed the Dick bill, which thoroughly revised the obsolete Militia Act of 1792. It separated the militia into two classes—the Organized Militia, to be known as the National Guard, and the Reserve Militia—and provided that, over a five-year period, the Guard's organization and equipment be patterned after that of the Regular Army. To help accomplish these changes in the Guard, the Dick bill made available federal funds; prescribed drill at least twice a month,

43

supplemented with short annual training periods; permitted detailing of Regular officers to Guard units; and directed holding of joint maneuvers each year. Failure of the new measure, however, to modify significantly the long-standing provisions that severely restricted federal power to call up Guard units and control Guard personnel limited its effectiveness. Subsequent legislation in 1908 and 1914 reduced these restrictions to some extent, giving the President the right to prescribe the length of federal service and, with the advice and consent of the Senate, to appoint all officers of the Guard while the Guard was in federal service.

Although the largest permanent unit of the Regular Army in peacetime continued to be the regiment, experience in the Spanish-American War, observation of new developments abroad, and lessons learned in annual maneuvers all testified to the need for larger, more self-sufficient units, composed of the combined arms. Beginning in 1905, the *Field Service Regulations* laid down a blueprint for the organization of divisions in wartime, and in 1910 the General Staff drew up a plan for three permanent infantry divisions to be composed of designated Regular Army and National Guard regiments. Because of trouble along the Mexican border in the spring of 1911, the plan was not carried out. Instead, the Army organized a provisional maneuver division, ordering its component units, consisting of three brigades comprised of nearly 13,000 officers and men, to concentrate at San Antonio, Texas. The division's presence there, it was hoped, would end the border disturbances.

The effort proved only how unready the Army was to mobilize quickly for any kind of national emergency. Assembly of the division required several months. The War Department had to collect Regular Army troops from widely scattered points in the continental United States and denude every post, depot, and arsenal to scrape up the necessary equipment. Even so, when the maneuver division finally completed its concentration in August 1911, it was far from fully operational, since none of its regiments were up to strength or adequately armed and equipped. Fortunately, the efficiency of the division was not put to any battle test, and within a short time it was broken up and its component units were returned to their home stations. Because those members of Congress who had Army installations in their own districts insisted on retaining them, the War Department was prevented from relocating units so that there would be a greater concentration of troops in a few places. The only immediate result of the Army's attempt to gain experience in the handling of large units was an effort to organize on paper the scattered posts of the Army so that their garrisons, which averaged 700 troops each, could join one of three divisions. But these abortive attempts to mobilize larger units were not entirely without value. In 1913 when the Army again had to strengthen the forces along the Mexican border, a division assembled in Texas in less than a week, ready for movement to any point where it might be needed.

Caribbean Problems and Projects

The close of the War with Spain brought no satisfactory solution for the Cuban problem. As a result of years of misrule and fighting, conditions on the island when the war ended were deplorable. Under provisions of the Teller amendment, the United States was pledged to turn over the rule of Cuba to its people. American forces, however, stayed on to assist the Cubans in achieving at least a modicum of economic and political stability. The first step was to set up a provisional government, headed in the beginning by Maj. Gen. John R. Brooke and later by General Wood. This government promptly undertook a program of rehabilitation and reform. An outstanding achievement was eliminating yellow fever, which had decimated Army troops during the war. Researchers and experiments carried out by the Army Medical Department culminated in the discovery that the dread disease is transmitted by a specific type of mosquito.

When order had been restored in Cuba, a constituent assembly met. Under the chairmanship of General Wood, it

45

drew up an organic law for the island patterned after the American Constitution. At the insistence of the United States, this law included several clauses known as the Platt amendment, which also appeared in the subsequent treaty concluded in 1903 by the two countries. The amendment limited the amount of debt Cuba could contract, granted the United States naval bases at Guantánamo and Bahia Honda, and gave the United States the right to intervene to preserve "Cuban independence" and maintain a government "adequate to the protection of life, property and individual liberty." In 1902, after a general election and the inauguration of the republic's first president, the Americans ended their occupation. But events soon demonstrated that the period of tutelage in self-government had been too short. In late 1906, when the Cuban Government proved unable to cope with a new rebellion, the United States intervened to maintain law and order. On the advice of Secretary of War Taft, President Roosevelt dispatched more than 5,000 troops to Havana, the so-called Army of Cuban Pacification, which remained in Cuba until early 1909. Again in 1912 and 1917, the United States found it necessary to intervene, but each time withdrew its occupying forces as soon as order was restored. Not until 1934 did the United States, consistent with its new Good Neighbor Policy, give up the right of intervention embodied in the Platt amendment.

Emergence of the United States as a world power with a primary concern for developments in the Caribbean Sea increased the long-time American interest in an isthmian canal. Discovery of gold in California in 1848 and the rapid growth of the west coast states had underlined the importance of developing a shorter sea route from Atlantic ports to the Pacific. The strategic need for a canal was dramatized for the American people during the Spanish-American War by the sixty-six-day voyage of the battleship *Oregon* from Puget Sound around Cape Horn to Santiago, where it joined the American Fleet barely in time to participate in the destruction of Cervera's ships.

A few months after the end of the War with Spain, McKinley told Congress that a canal under American control was "now more than ever indispensable." By the Hay-Pauncefote Treaty of 1901, the United States secured abrogation of the terms of the Clayton-Bulwer Treaty of 1850 that required the United States to share equally with Great Britain in construction and operation of any future isthmian canal. Finally, in 1903, the long-standing question of where the canal should be built—Nicaragua or Panama—was resolved in favor of Panama. An uprising in Panama against the government of Colombia provided President Roosevelt with an opportunity to send American naval units to support the rebels, assuring establishment of an independent republic. The new republic readily agreed to permit the United States to acquire control of a ten-mile strip across the isthmus, to purchase the property formerly belonging to the French syndicate that had attempted to construct a canal in the 1880's, and to build, maintain, and operate an interoceanic canal. Congress promptly appropriated the necessary funds for work to begin and the Isthmian Canal Commission set about investigating the problem of who should construct the canal.

When the commission advised the President that overseeing the construction of so vast a project was beyond the capabilities of any private concern, Roosevelt decided to turn the job over to the Army. He reorganized the commission, assigning to it new members—the majority were Army officers—and in 1907 appointed Col. George W. Goethals as its chairman and chief engineer. In this capacity, Goethals, a graduate of the Military Academy who had served in the Corps of Engineers since 1882, had virtually sole responsibility for administration of the canal project. Displaying great organizational ability, he overcame many serious difficulties, including problems of engineering, employee grievances, housing, and sanitation, to complete the canal by 1914. Goethals owed a part of his success to the support he received from the Army's Medical Department. Under the leadership of Col. William C. Gorgas, who earlier had played an important role in administering the sanitation program in Cuba, the Army carried through measures to control malaria and virtually wipe out yellow fever, ultimately

47

converting the Canal Zone into a healthy and attractive place to live and work.

The completed Panama Canal stood as a magnificent engineering achievement and an outstanding example of the Army's fulfillment of a peacetime mission; but its opening and operation under American administration were also highly significant from the point of view of military strategy. For the Navy, the Canal achieved economy of force by eliminating the necessity for maintaining large fleets in both the Atlantic and Pacific. For the Army, it created a new strategic point in the continental defense system that had to be strongly protected by the most modern fortifications manned by a large and well-trained garrison.

The Army on the Mexican Border

Early in the twentieth century, the Army found itself frequently involved in hemispheric problems, not only with the countries of the Caribbean region, but also with the United States' southern neighbor, Mexico. That nation, after a long era of relative political stability, entered a period of revolutionary turmoil. Beginning in 1911, internal conflicts in the northern part of the country led to recurrent incidents along the Mexican border, posing a serious threat to peace. President William Howard Taft first ordered strengthening of the border patrols and then, in the summer of 1911, concentration of the maneuver division at San Antonio. After a period of quiet, General Victoriano Huerta in 1913 deposed and replaced President Francisco Madero. The assassination of Madero shortly thereafter led to full-scale civil war between Huerta's forces and those of General Venustiano Carranza, leader of the so-called Constitutionalists, and Emiliano Zapata, chief of the radicals. Woodrow Wilson, who had succeeded Taft as President, disapproved of the manner in which Huerta had come to power. In a significant shift from traditional American policy, the President decided not to recognize Huerta on the grounds that his assumption of power did not meet the test of "constitu-

48

tional legitimacy." At the same time, Wilson imposed an arms embargo on both sides in the civil war. But in early 1914, when Huerta's forces halted the Constitutionalists, Wilson endeavored to help Carranza by lifting the embargo.

Resentment over Wilson's action contributed to the arrest in February of American sailors by followers of Huerta in the port of Tampico. Although they were soon released with an expression of regret from Huerta, Rear Adm. Henry T. Mayo, commanding the American Fleet in the area, demanded a public apology. Huerta refused. Feeling that intervention was unavoidable and seeing an opportunity to deprive Huerta of important ports, President Wilson supported Admiral Mayo and proposed to occupy Tampico, seize Veracruz, and blockade both ports. When a German steamer carrying a cargo of ammunition arrived unexpectedly at Veracruz in late April, the United States put ashore a contingent of marines and sailors to occupy the port and prevent unloading of the ship. Naval gunfire checked a Mexican counterattack and by the end of the month an American force of nearly 8,000—about half marines and half Army troops—under command of Maj. Gen. Frederick Funston occupied the city. For a time war with Mexico seemed inevitable, but both Wilson and Huerta accepted mediation and the Mexican leader agreed to resign. Carranza had barely had time to assume office when his erstwhile ally, Francisco "Pancho" Villa, rebelled and proceeded to gain control over most of northern Mexico.

Despite the precariousness of Carranza's hold on Mexico, President Wilson decided to recognize his government. It was now the turn of Villa to show resentment. He instigated a series of border incidents which culminated in a surprise attack by 500 to 1,000 of his men against Columbus, New Mexico, on March 9, 1916. Villa's troops killed a substantial number of American soldiers and civilians and destroyed considerable property before units of the 13th Cavalry drove them off. The following day, President Wilson ordered Brig. Gen. John J. Pershing into Mexico to assist the Mexican Government in capturing Villa.

On March 15 the advance elements of this punitive

49

GENERAL PERSHING AND HIS TROOPS *during the pursuit of Villa.*

expedition entered Mexico in "hot pursuit." For the next several months, Pershing's troops chased Villa through unfriendly territory for hundreds of miles, never quite catching up with him but managing to disperse most of his followers. Although Carranza's troops also failed to capture Villa, Carranza soon showed that he had no desire to have the United States do the job for him. He protested the continued presence of American troops in Mexico and insisted upon their withdrawal. Carranza's unfriendly attitude, plus orders from the War Department forbidding attacks on Mexicans who were not followers of Villa, made it difficult for Pershing to deal effectively with other hostile Mexicans who blocked his path without running the risk of precipitating war. Some clashes with Mexican Government troops actually occurred. The most important took place in June at Carrizal where scores were killed or wounded. This action once again created a critical situation and led President Wilson to call 75,000 National Guardsmen into federal service to help police the border.

Aware that the majority of Americans favored a peaceful solution, Wilson persuaded Carranza to resume diplomatic negotiations. The two leaders agreed in late July to submit the disputes arising out of the punitive expedition to a joint commission for settlement. Some time later the commission ruled that the American unit commander in the Carrizal affair was at fault. Although the commission broke up in January 1917 without reaching agreement on a plan for evacuating Pershing's troops, relations between the United States and Germany had reached so critical a stage that Wilson had no alternative but to order withdrawal of the punitive expedition.

Pershing failed to capture Villa, but the activities of the American troops in Mexico and along the border were not entirely wasted effort. Dispersal of Villa's band put an end to serious border incidents. More important, from a military point of view, was the intensive training in the field received by both Regular Army and National Guard troops who served on the border and in Mexico. Too, the partial mobilization drew further attention to the still unsolved problem of developing a satisfactory system for maintaining in peacetime the nucleus of those trained forces that would be required to supplement the Regular Army in national emergencies. Fortunately, many defects in the military establishment, especially in the National Guard, came to light in time to be corrected before the Army plunged into the war already under way in Europe.

CHAPTER 3

World War I: The First Three Years

As the armed camp that Europe had become by the summer of 1914 approached the point of explosion, the United States was markedly unprepared for any role that a European holocaust might create for the New World. Nor was there any widespread agitation to alter that situation, for despite the nation's increased involvement in world affairs, most Americans looked to the tactic of the ostrich to keep them out of the trouble. Americans, President Woodrow Wilson would admonish once war came, should remain "impartial in thought as well as in action."

Although the Navy, the nation's first line of defense, was the world's third largest, the Army was woefully inadequate for coping with anything much more complex than domestic disturbances or border defense. In striking contrast to 1.5 million trained men available in France and more than 2 million in Germany, the U.S. Army was short even the 100,000-man strength that Congress had authorized in 1902. Within the Army high command the contest of authority between the General Staff and the powerful bureau chiefs still went on, for all Elihu Root's reforms, and argument persisted over Emory Upton's rejection of the militia system in favor of the concept of an expansible army.

How War Came in Europe

The event that set off war in Europe came in late June at Sarajevo where a fanatical Serbian nationalist assassinated the heir to the Austro-Hungarian throne. In other times and under different conditions, this act might not have been enough to catapult the world into the most widespread and costly conflict man had yet known, one that eventually would put under arms sixty-five million men from thirty countries representing every continent, and one that would involve sea battles around the globe and major land campaigns not only in Europe but in parts of Africa and Asia Minor.

Yet as matters stood that summer of 1914, Europe was a tinderbox awaiting a spark. The situation was, in the words of President Wilson's personal adviser, Col. Edward M. House, "militarism run stark mad."

European nationalism had much to do with it. In Germany, a newly united nation forged from a loose-knit confederation of quarreling states no longer had the strong guiding hand of its able creator, Chancellor Otto von Bismarck, but instead had the chauvinistic direction of Wilhelm II, the kaiser. In Italy, also only recently united, vacillation and indecision reigned. In Russia, center of bellicose pan-Slavism, an autocratic czar already was feeling the pressure of people's revolt. In the Balkans, various minorities, particularly the Serbs, were challenging the patchwork amalgamation that was the Austro-Hungarian empire.

At the same time the industrial revolution, with its attendant commercial expansion, had prompted Germany to seek entry into the colonial system that long had been the province of France and Britain. As the Germans built the navy that was essential to their ambition, Britain's age-old supremacy of the seas was challenged. Germany's rise also threatened France on the ground, already tangibly demonstrated in the war of 1870-71, which produced in the French a lasting bitterness and such a burning desire to regain the lost provinces of Alsace and Lorraine that many saw a war of irredentism as inevitable.

The Germans continued to expand their military machine in keeping with their ever-growing aspirations, and as the French followed suit, an arms race of frightening proportions ensued. Meanwhile, the nations banded together in alliances designed to offset one another. There was at first the Triple Alliance composed of Germany, Austria, and Italy. On the other side, the Entente Cordiale between Britain and France gradually merged with the Dual Alliance of France and Russia to become the Triple Entente. With the defection of Italy, Germany and Austria became the Central Powers, which Bulgaria and Turkey eventually joined. The Triple Entente became, with the addition of Italy, the nucleus of the Allied Powers.

Despite some halfhearted efforts to localize the dispute over the assassinated prince, the fact that Russia backed Serbia and the kaiser promised Austria full support meant that the only real question was the date when the war was to begin. The answer to that came on July 28 when Austria declared war on Serbia. In view of the entangling alliances and the bulging arsenals, entry of all the major powers into the conflict was all but preordained.

The Early Campaigns

The bellicosity of Germany toward both Russia and France dictated for the Germans a two-front war. To meet this contingency, the German General Staff had laid its plans to defeat France swiftly before the Russians with their ponderous masses could fully mobilize, then to shift forces rapidly to the east and destroy the Russians at will.

The maneuver designed to defeat the French was the handiwork of Germany's gifted former Chief of Staff, Count Alfred von Schlieffen, who lent his name to the plan. Deducing that the French would attack in Alsace and Lorraine, Schlieffen proposed to trap them in a massive single envelopment, a great scythelike movement through the Low Countries and into northern France, thence west and south of Paris. Schlieffen was prepared to give ground

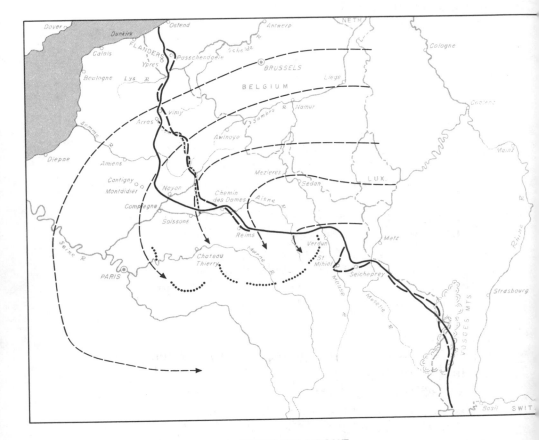

WESTERN FRONT
Sep 1914 – Mar 1918

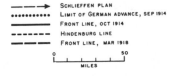

SCHLIEFFEN PLAN
LIMIT OF GERMAN ADVANCE, SEP 1914
FRONT LINE, OCT 1914
HINDENBURG LINE
FRONT LINE, MAR 1918

0   50
MILES

MAP 3

on his left wing in Alsace-Lorraine to insure keeping the French armies occupied until a powerful right wing—the tip of the scythe—could complete the envelopment. So basic to the plan was the power of the right wing that the old man reputedly stressed it in his dying words. *(Map 3)*

Schlieffen's successor, Helmuth von Moltke, failed to heed this proviso. Moltke eliminated the invasion of the Netherlands, thus confining the German right wing to a narrow fortified corridor on either side of the Belgian city of Liége. Wary of the theory of giving ground in Alsace-Lorraine, he shifted troops from the right to strengthen the defense on the left. Similarly worried about the strength of the German forces assigned to contain the Russians, Moltke withdrew four and a half corps from the right wing to move to the east.

These vagaries almost did in the Schlieffen plan, yet such surprise did the maneuver achieve that by late August French and British were in full retreat, the threat to Paris so real that the French Government abandoned the city. At that point Moltke again wavered, for word came that the Russians had mobilized far faster than expected and had begun to attack. Under pressure from the kaiser, Moltke again violated Schlieffen's dictum, pulling out two more corps from his right wing. In an effort to compensate for this diminution by reducing the depth of the envelopment, he ordered the tip of the scythe to pass east rather than west of Paris.

The two corps that Moltke withdrew had no effect in the east, since they arrived only after the Germans already had repelled the Russians in the battles of Tannenberg and the Masurian Lakes. Had Moltke retained them, they might not have been enough to carry the Schlieffen plan through to victory; but since their departure was what had prompted Moltke to alter the scope of the envelopment, their presence would have sharply changed the nature of what followed, the "Miracle of the Marne."

Paris spared, the French Commander in Chief, General Joseph Joffre, rallied the retreating French and British armies along the Marne east of the city, while in Paris the city's commander assembled the garrison—some of them transported in sputtering Parisian taxis—and hurled them against the German flank. That action afforded time for main British and French forces to turn, halt the Germans at the Marne River east of Paris, and drive them back to the Aisne River, forty miles to the north.

As stalemate developed along the Aisne, each side tried to envelop the northern flank of the other in successive battles that by October had extended the opposing lines all the way to the Belgian coast. The year would end with the Germans in control of most of Belgium and of the rich mining and industrial provinces of northern France, while the Allies, to their good fortune, managed to hold on to most of the Channel ports, which were vital if the British were to supply their troops on the Continent and if the Germans were to be denied critical bases for operations against the Royal Navy.

Hurting from unexpectedly brutal losses and stunned at the indecision of the first four months of warfare, Allied and German armies alike went to ground. The landscape from Switzerland to the sea soon was scarred with opposing systems of zigzag, timber-revetted trenches, fronted by tangles of barbed wire sometimes more than 150 feet deep and featured here and there by covered dugouts providing shelter for troops and horses and by observation posts in log bunkers or concrete turrets. Out beyond the trenches and the barbed wire was a muddy desert called no man's land where artillery fire had eliminated habitation and vegetation alike, where men in nighttime listening posts strained to hear what the enemy was about, and where rival patrols clashed.

It would eventually be apparent to both sides that they had miscalculated, that the newly developed machine gun and improved indirect fire artillery had bolstered not the offense but the defense, and that which had been presaged—but ignored—in the U.S. Civil War and in the Russo-Japanese War had come to be. The spade had become the *sine qua non* of the battlefield, lessening the applicability of such principles of war as maneuver, economy of force, surprise, and making critical the principle of mass. Masses of men—nearly 2 million Germans, 3 million Allied troops; masses of artillery—barrages lasted days and even weeks before an offensive; and masses of casualties—British and French in 1915 lost 1.5 million men killed, wounded, and missing. Yet through it all the opposing lines stood much as they had at the start. For more than two years they would vary less than ten miles in either direction.

To meet the high cost of the long, deadly struggle, the opposing powers turned more than ever before in history to the concept of the nation in arms. Even Britain, for so many years operating on the theory of a powerful navy and only a small though highly professional army, resorted to conscription and sent massive new armies to the Continent. To appease the appetite of the vast armies for munitions, equipment, and supplies, the nations harnessed their mines, factories, and railroads to war production, levied high income taxes, froze wages and prices, rationed food and other commodities.

On the battlefield, commanders persisted in a vain hope that somehow the stalemate might be ended and breakthrough and exploitation achieved. Although the Germans spent much of their effort in 1915 in a futile campaign for quick victory against the Russians, it was they who first came close to a breakthrough on the Western Front. They did so in April with a greenish mist of chlorine gas released from thousands of canisters against a French colonial division on the British sector of the front. The colonials broke, but the Germans were unprepared to exploit the advantage. The first use of poison gas thus was a strategic blunder, wasting total surprise for nothing more than local gains.

The British similarly blundered the next year when they also introduced a new weapon prematurely. This was the tank, an ungainly, ponderous offspring of a marriage of armor with the caterpillar tractor; it owed its name to British attempts to deceive the Germans that the vehicle was a water storage device. In the first commitment in September 1916, 34 tanks helped British infantry advance a painful mile and a half. There would be other attacks in later months involving tanks in strengths close to 500, but the critical element of surprise already had passed. Tanks later would prove sufficient to achieve the penetration everybody sought, but they were too slow and too subject to mechanical failure to fill the old role of horse cavalry as the tool of exploitation.

For all the lack of decision, both poison gas and the tank soon were established weapons, although the Germans were slow to accept the tank. Another weapon, meanwhile, found full acceptance on both sides: the airplane, frail forerunner of modern tactical and strategic bombers. Used at first primarily for reconnaissance, then as a counterreconnaissance weapon to fight the enemy's planes, and finally as an offensive weapon to attack ground troops, before the war ended aircraft engaged in strategic missions against railroads, factories, and cities, presaging the mass destruction that was to follow in another great war.

A fourth new weapon was the submarine, which the Germans employed with a ruthless skill that would bring them close to victory but would in the end provoke the instrument of their downfall. When the Germans first opened submarine warfare early in 1915, only 27 U-boats, as the submarines were called, were ready for action. Even this number quickly achieved impressive results, soon sinking more than 150,000 tons of Allied shipping each month. U-boat crews could not always correctly identify vessels which they attacked, and many neutral ships were sunk. The first American vessel to be involved was the merchant ship *Gulflight,* struck by a torpedo on the first day of May, but the event with sharpest impact on public opinion followed a week later when a submarine off the coast of Ireland sank the British liner *Lusitania,* with the loss of 1,198 lives, including 128 Americans.

The Impact of the War on the United States

The sinking of the *Lusitania* shocked an American public that, while unable to follow the President's dictum on impartiality of thought, had nevertheless displayed up to this point little desire to become directly involved in Europe's bloodbath. Although most Americans had from the first resented the submarine campaign, Britain too was violating the freedom of the seas with a blockade not only of Germany but of neutral European nations as well. This had raised the question of whether the acts of both sides were not equally reprehensible; but the heavy loss of life in the sinking of the *Lusitania* invoked fresh ire against the Germans. Membership in patriotic organizations flourished, and voices advocating preparedness found new listeners.

Among the voices were those of Elihu Root, ex-President Theodore Roosevelt, and former Secretary of War Henry L. Stimson. Another was that of General Wood, whose term as the Army's Chief of Staff had expired just over a year after President Wilson and his peace-oriented administration had come to office. Following a practice he had introduced while Chief of Staff of conducting summer camps where college students paying their own way could receive military training, Wood lent his support to a similar four-week camp for business and professional men at Plattsburg Barracks, New York. Known as the "Plattsburg idea," its success justified opening other camps, assuring a relatively small but influential cadre possessing basic military skills and imbued with enthusiasm for preparedness.

Yet these were voices of a heavily industrialized and articulate east. Few like them were to be heard from the rural south, the west, or a strongly isolationist midwest, where heavy settlements of German-Americans (called by some, derisively, "hyphenated Americans") detected in the talk of preparedness a heavy leaning toward the nation's historic Anglo-Saxon ties. There was in the country, too, a strong tide of outright pacifism, which possessed an eloquent spokesman in Wilson's Secretary of State, William Jennings Bryan.

How deep were Bryan's convictions became apparent in the government's reaction to the sinking of the *Lusitania*. Although Bryan agreed with the President's first diplomatic protest over the sinking, he dissented when the President, dissatisfied with the German reply and determined to insist

61

on the right of neutrals to engage in commerce on the high seas, insisted on a second and stronger note. The Secretary resigned.

Although sinkings by submarine continued through the summer of 1915, Wilson's persistent protest at last produced an apparent diplomatic victory when in September the Germans promised that passenger liners would be sunk only after warning and with proper safeguards for passengers' lives. Decelerating their campaign, the Germans actually acted less in response to American protests than to a realization that they lacked enough submarines to achieve victory by that means.

American commerce with Europe meanwhile continued, particularly in munitions, but because of the British blockade almost all was with the Allied nations. The British intercepted ships carrying foodstuffs to Germany and held them until their cargoes rotted. Just after mid-1915 they put even cotton on a long list of contraband and blacklisted any U.S. firm suspected of trading with the Central Powers. These were deliberate and painful affronts, but so profitable was the munitions trade that only the southern states, hurt by the loss of markets for cotton, raised loud protest. In October 1915 President Wilson repealed a ban earlier imposed on loans to belligerents, thereby further stimulating trade with the Allies.

While Americans as a whole remained opposed to entering the war, their sympathy for the Allied cause grew. A combination of Allied propaganda and German ineptitude was largely responsible. The propagandists were careful to insure that nobody forgot the German violation of Belgian neutrality, the ordeal of "Little Belgium." Stories of babies mutilated and women violated by German soldiers were rampant. The French executed nine women as spies during the war, but it was the death of a British nurse, Edith Cavell, at the hands of the Germans that the world heard about and remembered. Clumsy German efforts at propaganda in the United States backfired when two military attachès were discovered financing espionage and sabotage. The Germans did their cause no further good when one of their sub-marines in October 1916 surfaced in Newport Harbor, sent an officer ashore to deliver a letter for the German ambassador, then submerged and sank nine Allied ships close off the New England coast.

Continuing to champion neutrality and seeking—however unsuccessfully—to persuade the belligerents to establish international rules of submarine warfare, President Wilson was personally becoming more aware of the necessity for military preparedness. Near the end of a nationwide speaking tour in February 1916, he not only called for creation of "the greatest navy in the world" but also urged widespread military training for civilians, lest some day the nation be faced with "putting raw levies of inexperienced men onto the modern field of battle." Still upholding the cause of freedom of the seas, he refused to go along with congressmen who sought to forbid Americans to travel on armed merchant ships.

Wilson nevertheless continued to demonstrate a fervent hope for neutrality. A submarine attack in March on the French steamer *Sussex* with Americans aboard convinced the President's adviser, Colonel House, and his new Secretary of State, Robert Lansing, that the nation should sever diplomatic relations with Germany, a course that a fiery speech of self-justification by the German chancellor in the Reichstag and a cynical reply to an American note of protest did nothing to discourage. Wilson instead went only so far as to dispatch what amounted to an ultimatum, demanding that the Germans cease the submarine war against passenger and merchant vessels or face severance of relations with the United States.

While questioning the American failure to deal as sternly with the British blockade and rejecting the charge of unrestricted submarine warfare, Germany again agreed to conform to American demands for prior warning and for protecting the lives of passengers. Wilson, in turn, saw that unless something could be done about the British blockade the German vow probably would be shortlived. When a protest to the British availed nothing, the President offered the services of the United States to negotiate a peace. That brought little positive response from either side.

The National Defense Act of 1916

Some of the President's growing sympathy for the cause of preparedness could be traced to increasing concern on the part of members of his administration, most notably the Secretary of War, Lindley M. Garrison. As an annex to the Secretary's annual report in September 1915, Garrison had submitted a study prepared by the General Staff entitled, "A Proper Military Policy for the United States." Like proposals for reform advanced earlier by Stimson and Wood, the new study turned away from the Uptonian idea of an expansible Regular Army, which Root had favored, to the more traditional American concept of a citizen army as the keystone of an adequate defense force. Garrison proposed more than doubling the Regular Army, increasing federal support for the National Guard, and creating a new 400,000-man volunteer force to be called the Continental Army, a trained reserve under federal control as opposed to the state control of the Guard.

Although Wilson refused to accept more than a small increase in the Regular Army, he approved the concept of a Continental Army. Garrison's proposal drew support, too, in the Senate, but not enough to overcome adamant opposition in the House of Representatives from strong supporters of the National Guard. Influential congressmen countered with a bill requiring increased federal responsibility for the Guard, acceptance of federal standards, and agreement by the Guard to respond to a Presidential call to service. Under pressure from these congressmen, Wilson switched his support to the Congressional plan. This, among other issues, prompted Garrison to resign.

There the matter might have bogged down had not Pancho Villa shot up Columbus, New Mexico. Facing pressing requirements for the National Guard on the Mexican border, the two halls of Congress at last compromised, incorporating the concept of the citizen army as the foundation of the American military establishment but not in the form of a Continental Army. They sought instead to make the National Guard the nucleus of the citizen force.

Passed in May and signed into law the next month, the bill was known as the National Defense Act of 1916. It provided for an army in no way comparable to those of the European combatants and produced cries of outrage from those still subscribing to the Uptonian doctrine. It also contained a severe restriction inserted by opponents of a strong General Staff, sharply limiting the number of officers who could be detailed to serve on the staff at the same time in or near Washington. The bill represented nevertheless the most comprehensive military legislation yet enacted by the U.S. Congress.

The National Defense Act of 1916 authorized an increase in the peacetime strength of the Regular Army over a period of five years to 175,000 men and a wartime strength of close to 300,000. Bolstered by federal funds and federal-stipulated organization and standards of training, the National Guard was to be increased more than fourfold to a strength of over 400,000 and obligated to respond to the call of the President. The act also established both an Officers' and an Enlisted Reserve Corps and a Volunteer Army to be raised only in time of war. Additional officers were to be trained in colleges and universities under a Reserve Officers' Training Corps program.

Going beyond the heretofore recognized province of military legislation, the National Defense Act of 1916 also granted power to the President to place orders for defense materials and to force industry to comply. The act further directed the Secretary of War to conduct a survey of all arms and munitions industries. A few months later the Congress demonstrated even greater interest in the industrial aspects of defense by creating a civilian Council of National Defense made up of leaders of industry and labor, supported by an advisory commission composed of the secretaries of the principal government departments, and charged with the mission of studying economic mobilization. The administration furthered the preparedness program by creating a U.S. Shipping Board to regulate sea transport while developing a naval auxiliary fleet and a merchant marine.

The War in 1916

As Wilson, through the fall of 1916, waged a campaign for re-election on a peace platform, the war on the Western Front remained a stalemate despite two of history's greatest and bloodiest battles. In a switch of main effort from Eastern to Western Front, Moltke's successor as Chief of the General Staff, Erich von Falkenhayn, chose the fortress town of Verdun, which he deemed of immense moral and psychological significance to France, for massive attack in a campaign designed to bleed France white. There followed the Battle of the Somme in which the British with French support attacked in quest of breakthrough and victory. Neither achieved much more than to run up the casualty total: 460,000 French at Verdun, 300,000 German; 614,000 Allied troops on the Somme, 650,000 German.

The appalling carnage of these battles brought the relief of Falkenhayn, replaced by the heroes of the Eastern Front, Paul von Hindenburg as Chief of the General Staff, and Erich Ludendorff as First Quartermaster General, his deputy, although it was Ludendorff rather than the aging Hindenburg who dominated in this command arrangement. It also wrote the end to the field career of the French Commander in Chief, Field Marshal Joffre. In England, a government fell.

On the Eastern Front, the Russians had rallied after giving up Poland to the Germans and struck back with a major offensive against the Austrians that carried almost to the passes leading through the Carpathian Mountains. It was the greatest Russian victory of the war, but it cost a million men and left the poorly armed, poorly equipped Russian soldier ready to embrace revolution.

That year, too, Italians and Austrians ground each other

down along the Isonzo in northeastern Italy, while an adventure in peripheral warfare, launched the preceding year at the instigation of Winston Churchill, First Lord of the Admiralty, ended indecisively in evacuation of the Gallipoli peninsula. Indecisive too was the war's greatest sea battle, when a cornered German surface fleet ventured out of the Baltic to meet the British Fleet in the Battle of Jutland, then withdrew to the corner for the rest of the war, but only after inflicting more losses than it received.

During the last three months of 1916, the German submarine campaign again mounted in intensity. Each month the British lost 176,000 tons of shipping. Counting Allied and neutral shipping, the losses averaged 192,000 tons a month, a shocking increase over the previous year that reflected a continuing growth of the U-boat fleet.

An End to Neutrality

As a new year of war opened, German leaders decided that they had lost so many men at Verdun and on the Somme that they would have to assume the defensive on the Western Front; their only hope of quick victory lay with the submarines, of which they now had close to 200. By operating an unrestricted campaign against all shipping, whatever the nationality, in waters off the British Isles and France, the Germans believed they could defeat the Allies within six months. While they recognized the strong risk of bringing the United States into the war by this tactic, they believed they could starve the Allies into submission before the Americans could raise, train, and deploy an Army.

The German ambassador in Washington continued to encourage Wilson to pursue his campaign for peace even as the Germans made their U-boats ready. On January 31, 1917, Germany informed the U.S. Government and other neutrals that beginning the next day U-boats would sink all vessels, neutral and Allied alike, without warning.

While the world waited to learn the American reaction, President Wilson searched for some alternative to war.

Three days later, still groping desperately for a path to peace, he went before the Congress, not to ask a declaration of war, but to announce a break in diplomatic relations. This step, Wilson hoped, would be enough to turn the Germans from their new course.

Wilson could not know it at the time but an intelligence intercept already had placed in British hands a German telegram that, when released, would remove any doubt as to German intentions toward the United States. This message was sent in January from the German Foreign Secretary, Arthur Zimmermann, to the German ambassador to Mexico, proposing that in the event of war with the United States, Germany and Mexico conclude an alliance, with the adherence of Japan. In exchange for Mexico's taking up arms against the United States, Germany would provide generous financial assistance. Victory achieved, Mexico was to regain her lost territory of Texas, New Mexico, and Arizona.

Cognizant of the impact the message was bound to have on the United States, the British were nevertheless slow to release it; they had to devise a method to assure the Americans of its authenticity while concealing from the Germans that they had broken the German diplomatic code. On February 23, just over a month after intercepting the telegram, the British turned over a copy to the American ambassador in London.

When President Wilson received the news, he was angered but still unprepared to accept it as cause for war. In releasing the message to the press, he had in mind not inciting the nation to war but instead moving Congress to pass a bill authorizing the arming of American merchant ships, most of which were standing idle in American ports because of the submarine menace. As with the break in diplomatic relations, this, the President hoped, would so impress the Germans that they would abandon their unrestricted submarine campaign.

Although Congress and most of the nation were shocked by revelation of the Zimmermann message, their hopes for neutrality shattered, pacifists and pro-Germans countered with a roar of disbelief that the message was authentic. Zimmermann himself silenced them when in Berlin he admitted having sent the telegram.

In the next few weeks, four more American ships fell victim to German U-boats. Fifteen Americans died. At last convinced that the step was inevitable, the President went before Congress late on April 2 to ask for a declaration of war. Four days later, on April 6, 1917, the United States declared war on Germany.

A Year of Crisis in Europe

The United States entered the war even as Allied fortunes were approaching their nadir.

In Russia in March a spontaneous revolution had erupted, prompting the czar to abdicate and initiating a struggle for power between moderate Socialists and hard-core revolutionaries, the Bolsheviks. The moderates won, formed a provisional government, and vowed to continue the war, a development that made going to war more palatable to many Americans, since the overthrow of the old dynastic-imperial system gave logic to a Wilsonian phrase that this was a war "to make the world safe for democracy."

The reign of the moderates was destined to be brief, partly because the Germans contrived to foment trouble by permitting an exiled revolutionary leader, Nikolai Lenin, to pass from Switzerland through Germany in a special train to Russia. There Lenin joined with other leaders, including Leon Trotsky, in an open campaign to upset the moderate government. As forces of the Central Powers launched a counteroffensive in July close behind a short-lived Russian offensive, Russian units, riven by revolutionary cells, collapsed, with soldiers deserting by the tens of thousands. The way was prepared for the Bolsheviks to seize power in the October Revolution. The new government under Lenin and Trotsky sued for peace.

On the Western Front the year's operations began with great expectations on the Allied side as a new French commander, General Robert Nivelle, prepared a grandiose, end-the-war offensive. With support from a converging British attack from the north, Nivelle planned to send four French armies to cut in behind a great bulge in the line between Soissons and Arras. Unfortunately, Nivelle was too open with his preparations. The Germans moved first, pulling back from the bulge to a previously prepared position which the Allies would name the Hindenburg Line. In the process they laid waste to the land behind them, and in occupying a shorter line gained 13 divisions for their reserve. In exchange for the usual minor gains, the British incurred 84,000 casualties, the French 187,000.

The worst was still to come. Mutiny broke out in one French regiment and spread swiftly through 54 divisions. The government relieved Nivelle, putting in his place to restore the Army's morale and discipline Henri Philippe Pétain, who had emerged as the hero of the earlier battle for Verdun.

With the French temporarily *hors de combat*, the British took up the struggle with a giant offensive in Flanders. First came a limited objective attack to straighten a minor bulge in the line known as the Messines Ridge. Working like moles, the British dug five miles of underground tunnels, laid a million pounds of explosives, then literally blew up the Messines Ridge. With some 20,000 Germans killed or wounded in one blow, the British took the ridge; but when they launched their main offensive a few miles to the north, breakthrough was as elusive as ever. In a battle that persisted into late fall—Passchendaele, they called it, after a ridge that was the first objective—British casualties totaled 245,000, German half that number.

More disastrous still were the results of an Austrian offensive launched with German assistance in Italy in the fall. In what became known as the Battle of Caporetto, the Italians in one blow lost 305,000 men; 275,000 of them surrendered as the Army fell back a hundred miles in panic. British and French divisions had to be rushed to Italy to keep the Italians in the war.

A combination of all these crises prompted the Allied

governments to strive seriously for the first time to create some form of unified command. Yet for all the peril, no government was yet prepared to yield its troops to foreign command. The Allies created a Supreme War Council with both political and military representation from all the Allied nations, a step toward an over-all command, but only a step.

Despite the seriousness of the crises on land, the most portentous of all as the United States entered the war was the crisis at sea. In February 1917 alone, German U-boats had sunk 781,000 tons of Allied and neutral shipping, and the British were predicting a loss in April of almost 900,000 tons. At this rate, the British reckoned, the Germans soon would force them out of the war; by October 1917, the end would be in sight.

The United States Prepares for War

Although far from ready for war, the U.S. Navy fortunately was in a position to take immediate steps to aid the Allies. An emissary from Washington, Rear Adm. William S. Sims, helped to convince the British Admiralty to employ a new tactic to counter the rampaging submarines, a system of convoys whereby destroyers and other warships escorted groups of merchant vessels across the Atlantic. By early May, 6 U.S. destroyers had begun to participate in this system, and before the summer was out the number would grow to 37, while 5 U.S. battleships were operating in European waters.

The convoy system did not defeat the submarine, but it was effective enough to break the crisis. During the last half of 1917 total ship sinkings declined steadily; in December less than 400,000 tons of shipping was lost. In the meantime, the United States had joined Britain in a massive shipbuilding program.

The U.S. Army was in no position to make its weight felt immediately. Counting that part of the National Guard federalized for duty on the Mexican border, the Army numbered only 210,000 men with an additional 97,000

Guardsmen still in state service. Not a single unit of divisional size existed and so hobbled by the restriction written into the National Defense Act was the General Staff that only 19 officers were on duty in the headquarters in Washington. Although the experience in Mexico had given the little Army some seasoning, the main result of that involvement had been to point up shortages in equipment and other deficiencies. Except for 890,000 Springfield rifles, the Army's arsenal was nearly bare.

Given the state of the Army and the fact that the United States went to war over the limited issue of unrestricted submarine warfare, the nation conceivably might have confined its contribution to the war at sea, but such a concept received neither general nor official support. Starting with the President's war message to Congress, the intent was to send ground troops to Europe and to do all possible to defeat the German empire and end the war.

Congress, the President, the government moved swiftly in that direction. The House of Representatives authorized a $7 billion bond issue; to build up and manage the merchant marine, the President created the Emergency Fleet Corporation; the Treasury Department opened a drive to float a $2 billion Liberty Loan. The Army General Staff, meanwhile, quickly decided that to bolster Allied morale a division should be shipped as promptly as possible to France as tangible evidence that the United States intended to fight.

Forming a division required collecting as a nucleus four infantry regiments from the Mexican border, building them up to strength with men from other regiments and with recruits, and calling Reserve officers to fill out the staffs. By mid-June the 1st Infantry Division had begun to embark amid dockside confusion not unlike that in the Spanish-American War. Not only did the men lack many of their weapons but a large number had never even heard of some of them. Yet the pertinent fact was that a division was on the way to provide a much-needed boost for the war-weary Allied nations. On the Fourth of July, a battalion of the 16th Infantry marched through Paris to French cheers of near delirium, but it would be months before the 1st Division would be sufficiently trained to participate in the war even on a quiet sector of the front.

To command the American Expeditionary Forces, President Wilson chose the man with command experience in Mexico, John J. Pershing, even though Pershing was junior to five other major generals in the Army. Within three weeks of the appointment, Pershing was on his way to France to survey the situation and furnish the War Department with an estimate of the forces that would have to be provided. He was present for the 16th Infantry's parade on the Fourth of July and participated in a ceremony at the tomb of General Lafayette, where a Quartermaster colonel—not Pershing, as many would long believe—uttered the words, "Lafayette, we are here."

As Pershing was preparing to sail for Europe, Congress in mid-May passed a Selective Service Act based on a plan developed by the War Department after careful study of conscription in the Civil War. It was a model act, one that eliminated such inequities as substitutes, purchased exemptions, and bounties, and assured that conscripts would serve for the duration of the emergency. To spare the Army any opprobrium connected with administering the draft, this was made the responsibility of local civilian boards. Although these local boards were empowered to grant selective exemptions based on essential occupations and family obligations, all males between the ages of 21 and 30 had to register. These ages later were extended from 18 to 45.

The Selective Service Act also established the broad outlines of the Army's structure. There were to be three increments: (1) the Regular Army, to be raised immediately to the full wartime strength of 286,000 authorized in the National Defense Act of 1916; (2) the National Guard, also to be expanded immediately to the authorized strength of approximately 450,000; and (3) a National Army (the National Defense Act had called it a Volunteer Army), to be created in two increments of 500,000 men each at such time as the President should determine.

Much of the identity of these three segments eventually would be lost as recruits and draftees alike were absorbed in

73

all units, so that in mid-1918 the War Department would change the designation of all land forces to one "United States Army." The original segment to which regiments, brigades, and divisions belonged nevertheless continued to be apparent from numerical designations. For the Regular Army, for example, divisions were numbered up to 25, while numbers 26 through 75 were reserved for the National Guard and higher numbers for divisions of the National Army.

Just how large an army the United States was to raise depended in large measure on the situation in Europe and on General Pershing's recommendations from his vantage point there. Soon after Pershing's arrival in France, he called for approximately a million men to be sent to France before the end of 1918. This was the smallest number, Pershing noted, that would afford an independent fighting force, a full field army of 20 divisions and necessary supporting troops. This number, Pershing warned, probably would constitute only a start.

The War Department in turn translated Pershing's recommendation into a plan to send instead by the end of 1918 30 divisions with supporting services, a total of 1,372,000 men; but so disastrous were the developments in Europe in succeeding months—the Nivelle offensive, Passchendaele, Caporetto, the Russian Revolution—that Pershing felt impelled to revise his estimate. In June 1918, he would ask for 3,000,000 men with 66 divisions to be in France by May 1919. This figure he quickly raised to an estimate of 80 divisions by April 1919, followed shortly by a request for 100 divisions by July of the same year.

Although the War Department questioned whether 100 divisions could be sent to France by the summer of 1919 and even whether that many would be necessary to win the war, detailed study produced a promise to raise 98 divisions and to have 80 of them in France by the summer of 1919. This meant, in turn, an increase in the original program of 30 divisions by the end of 1918, raising the goal to 52 divisions.

Part of the War Department's concern was based on the size of the U.S. division—28,000 men—almost double that of

74

Allied and German divisions, which meant in numbers of men that 100 U.S. divisions were the equivalent of almost 200 Allied divisions. This size was a result of one of Pershing's early recommendations, which, along with advice of military missions sent from France and Britain, prompted radical changes in organization of the U.S. infantry division.

The need, as Pershing saw it, was for a division large enough to provide immense striking and staying power, one larger in size than most army corps of the Civil War. As determined by the War Department, the division was to be organized in 2 infantry brigades of 2 regiments each, a field artillery brigade with 1 heavy and 2 light regiments, a regiment of combat engineers, 3 machine gun battalions, plus signal, medical, and other supporting troops.

As the war proceeded, the Army actually would reach a peak strength of 3,685,458. This included 62 divisions, 43 of which were sent overseas. On this basis, when the war came to an end, the Army was running close to the projected goal of 52 divisions to be in France by the end of 1918.

How fast the Army could expand at the start depended in large measure on the availability of housing and of arms, equipment, and supplies. New Regular regiments and small units were organized immediately, using existing housing facilities, while the new National Guard formations were called in two increments and housed in tent camps, mainly in warmer southern states. Although over nine million men registered for the draft in June, the first would be called to fill the divisions of the National Army only in September after a priority building program could provide the first of the vast new cantonments that would be required. A special Cantonment Division of the Quartermaster Corps worked with a civilian Committee on Emergency Construction to provide these facilities.

In the matter of arms, munitions, and equipment, the demands were so urgent and so tremendous, not only for the Army but also for the Navy and the Allies, that as the authors of the National Defense Act of 1916 had anticipated, and as the European powers early had discovered, industry too had to be mobilized. For this task, the Council of National Defense as created by the National Defense Act provided a central planning office and control. The council early established a Munitions Standards Board, composed of industrialists to determine standards for munitions manufacturers, which grew by stages into a War Industries Board with broad powers to co-ordinate all purchasing by agencies of the Army and Navy, to establish production priorities, to create new plans and convert existing plants to priority uses, and to co-ordinate the activities of various civilian war agencies.

Despite these efforts, the demand for arms was so immense and immediate and the time required for contracts to be let and industry to retool so lengthy that the Army for a long time would have to train with obsolete and even wooden guns and in the end would have to depend heavily on Allied manufacture. The one weapon providing no particular problem was the rifle. To add to already existing stocks, the Army's own arsenals increased production of Springfields, while plants that had been filling Allied orders modified the British Lee-Enfield rifle to take U.S. ammunition for use by U.S. troops. All American units reaching France during the first year had to be equipped with Allied machine guns and automatic rifles, but new and excellent Browning machine guns and automatic rifles began coming off U.S. production lines in volume by mid-1918. Of some 2,250 artillery pieces used by American forces in France, only a hundred were of U.S. manufacture. Similarly an embryonic U.S. Tank Corps used French tanks, and in some instances British and French tank battalions supported U.S. troops. The Air Section that expanded rapidly to 11,425 flying officers, of whom 5,000 reached France, also had to depend primarily on planes provided by the Allies. The United States did produce a good 12-cylinder Liberty airplane engine, and a few U.S. planes saw service in latter weeks of the war.

The record of U.S. industry was somewhat better in terms of the soldier's personal needs, including his food. The Army worked closely with a War Food Administration to avoid the food scandals of earlier wars. Inductions had to be

76

GRAND REVIEW, CAMP DEVENS, MASSACHUSETTS.

slowed briefly until sufficient uniforms could be accumulated, and shortages in some items persisted, but as a result less of industry's failures than of a cumbersome Quartermaster contracting system, which was eventually corrected. The Army in any case made extensive purchases abroad but mainly in bulky items to relieve the burden on transatlantic shipping—horses, coal, lumber for overseas camps, and a few textile items like blankets.

Providing officers for the new divisions was another factor affecting the speed fo the Army's expansion, for at the start the Army had only 9,000 officers against an immediate requirement of 200,000. Although the General Staff at first contemplated scattering the officers and noncommissioned officers of the Regular Army to form cadres for the National Army, in keeping with Uptonian doctrine, it early became apparent that the small number of Regulars would be submerged and lost in the sea of conscripts. This was one of the factors influencing the General Staff's decision to form a division of Regulars for early shipment to France.

Eschewing the obvious though questionable expedient of appointing officers directly from civilian life, the Army provided direct commissions only for specialists like doctors and those uniquely qualified by civilian experience for the technical services. As a start, the Army conducted sixteen Officers' Training Camps for civilians and reservists on the order of the old "Plattsburg idea"; but in the main the Army drew its officers from the ranks of qualified enlisted men in the Regular Army, from the Reserve Officers' Training Corps and a Student Army Training Corps in colleges and universities, and in the largest numbers of all from Officers' Training Camps in division cantonments and later eight consolidated Officers' Training Schools. Officer candidates were admitted to these schools only after careful screening and then were given three months of intensive training. The 60 percent who made the grade were commissioned in the new National Army. Called in some circles "90-day wonders," these officers nevertheless provided the Army with a leadership far surpassing that of the average new officer in any previous war.

1ST. LT. EDWARD V. RICKENBACKER, FIRST AMERICAN
ACE, *with his Spad plane, France, 1918.*

How much training time the soldier needed before going overseas was long a matter of conjecture, but the War Department finally settled on four months' training in the United States. This was so rudimentary, particularly since the units with which the individual soldier went to war were similarly inexperienced, that General Pershing set up a thorough training course for all divisions once they arrived in France. Conducted with British and French assistance, Pershing's program was so lengthy as to provoke impatience on the part of the Allies and criticism on the part of many American officers.

Getting the troops to their training centers, then to ports of embarkation, and finally across the Atlantic was such a mammoth undertaking and had to be executed on such an emergency basis that confusion and mismanagement could hardly have been unexpected. To co-ordinate rail transportation, the government established a Railway War Board, which later became the Railroad Administration, but so congested did the railroads become that the government eventually seized and ran them through the Railroad Administration. The Shipping Board that had been created close on adoption of the National Defense Act of 1916 had had more time for preparation, but shipping nevertheless remained a critical item and ports often were glutted with supplies. The government cut imports drastically to conserve shipping, established a mass construction program of standardized cargo vessels, and seized interned German vessels and a few others of foreign registry; but British vessels still had to handle much of the traffic.

Changes in the Army High Command

As expansion and overseas deployment proceeded, the unprecedented and in some cases overwhelming demands of the situation had an inevitable impact on many of the Army's historic institutions. The most marked and at the same time of the most import for the future was on the organization of the General Staff and the authority of the Chief of Staff.

The office of the Chief of Staff had yet to find an assertive incumbent until early in March 1918, when the War Department brought back from France Pershing's artillery commander, Maj. Gen. Peyton C. March. In recalling March, the Secretary of War, Newton D. Baker, had reorganization of the General Staff specifically in mind, for a recent Senate investigation of quartermaster, supply, and transportation problems had focused attention on deficiencies that the early months of expansion had revealed.

In the Overman Act, passed by the Congress in May 1918, which granted the President broad authority to reorganize executive agencies during the war emergency, March obtained the tool needed to establish at long last General Staff authority over the heretofore powerful bureau chiefs. Given the additional authority of the rank of full general, March decreed that these chiefs were subordinate to the General Staff and were to report to the Secretary of War only through the Chief of Staff.

Drastically reorganizing the General Staff, March created four main divisions: Operations; Military Intelligence; Purchase, Storage, and Traffic; and War Plans. The titles fairly well explained the functions, except that Operations and War Plans shared the functions of the former War College Division and that Purchase, Storage, and Traffic provided the Army for the first time a central control over logistics. Under this reorganization, the total military and civilian strength of the General Staff increased to just over a thousand.

Lest there remain any room for misinterpreting the role of the Chief of Staff, March, with Secretary Baker's support, issued general orders spelling out the authority in specific terms. The order read, in part:

The Chief of Staff by law (Act of May 12, 1917) takes rank and precedence over all officers of the Army, and by virtue of that position and by authority of and in the name of the Secretary of War he issues such orders as will insure that the policies of the War Department are harmoniously executed by the several corps, bureaus, and other agencies of the Military Establishment and that the Army program is carried out speedily and efficiently.

That, in theory, completed at last the reform of the General Staff that Elihu Root had started, but in practice, an obstacle remained in the person of the field commander in France, General Pershing, who had been promoted to four-star rank ahead of March. Pershing had gone to France with an almost total authority to do the job as he saw it, and, despite technical subordination to March, Pershing resisted any effort by the Chief of Staff to assert authority over his command. The Secretary of War on a number of occasions had to act as arbiter between the two and, in matters related to the American Expeditionary Forces, usually acceded to Pershing's will rather than March's.

The final evolvement of the Chief of Staff as the incontestably supreme military chief of the Army would have to await Pershing's return and his assumption of the job himself, yet Peyton C. March stood, along with Root, as a primary architect of the position.

CHAPTER 4

World War I: The
U.S. Army Overseas

Included in the orders General Pershing received from the
Secretary of War before he left for France was a stipulation
"to cooperate with the forces of the other countries . . . but
in so doing the underlying idea must be kept in view that the
forces of the United States are a separate and distinct
component of the combined forces, the identity of which
must be preserved." This was a requirement that influenced
many of Pershing's early decisions in regard to the American
Expeditionary Forces and was to be for long months a
recurring source of contention between Pershing and Allied
commanders who were nearing the end of their manpower
resources.

Training and Organizing U.S. Troops

For assembling American troops, Pershing chose the
region southeast of Paris. Since the British were committed
to that part of the front north of Paris and since the French
had achieved their greatest concentration in protection of
the capital, they had tied up the Channel ports and the
railroads north and northeast of Paris. By locating southeast
of the city, U.S. forces would be close to the Lorraine

portion of the front, a likely spot for committing an independent American force. The French had few troops there and important objectives lay within reasonable striking distance—coal and iron mines and railroads vital to the Germans. This part of the front could be served by the ports of southern and southwestern France and by rail lines less committed to French and British requirements. Pershing set up his headquarters near the source of the Marne in Chaumont.

To Pershing, the training not only of the hastily assembled 1st Division but also of the others that followed before the end of 1917 (the 2d—half Regular Army, half Marine; 26th—New England National Guard; and 42d—called the "Rainbow Division" because it was a composite of Guardsmen from many states) was seriously inadequate. Many of the men in these divisions were recruits, replacements for those pulled out to help train newly forming units.

Pershing devised an intensive training schedule for the 1st Division and planned to follow a similar program for the other three with the idea of withholding all four from active sectors until all were ready, whereupon, late in 1918, they might be committed as the nucleus of an independent American force. Reinforced by other units arriving in 1918, Pershing in 1919 could open an offensive aimed at victory.

For training in trench warfare, Pershing gratefully accepted the help of experienced Allied officers. He also followed the Allied system of setting up special training centers and schools to teach subjects such as gas warfare, demolitions, and the use of the hand grenade and the mortar. Yet in the belief that the French and British had become too imbued with trench warfare to the exclusion of the open maneuvers that eventually would be necessary to achieve victory, he insisted on additional training in offensive tactics, including detailed work in rifle marksmanship and use of the bayonet.

Not until late October 1917 did Pershing submit the Ist Division to trial experience in the line. One battalion at a time from each regiment spent ten days with a French division. The first U.S. Army casualties of the war resulted from this deployment when early in November the Germans staged a trench raid against the same battalion that had paraded in Paris. With a loss of 3 of their own men, the Germans killed 3 Americans and captured 11.

The cycle in the trenches completed, Pershing submitted the 1st Division to further training to correct the deficiencies observed at the front. Only in mid-January of 1918, six months after its arrival in France, was the division ready in Pershing's view to move as a unit into a quiet sector of the trenches.

General Pershing had in the meantime been setting up the staff and logistical organization for managing the growing American force. Reflecting a strong similarity to the French system, his General Staff ultimately included a chief of staff, a deputy chief, and five assistant Chiefs supervising five sections: G-1 (Personnel), G-2 (Intelligence), G-3 (Operations), G-4 (Supply), and G-5 (Training). Staffs for divisions and later for corps and armies followed a similar organization, while to fill the new staff positions Pershing set up a General Staff College with a 3-month course.

To provide logistical support, Pershing created a Line of Communications under a single commander responsible directly to him. It was organized into base sections, each with one or more ports, an intermediate section for storage and classification of supplies, and an advanced section for distribution to the zone of operations. After American units entered combat, depots in the advanced section made up supplies for each division in trains which moved to division railheads, whence the divisions moved the supplies to the front in wagons and trucks. The designation Line of Communications was later changed to Services of Supply under command of Pershing's original chief of staff, Maj. Gen. James G. Harbord.

Pressure From French and British

Carrying out the comprehensive training program required all the determination at Pershing's disposal, for once the first exultation accompanying the arrival of American troops in France had predictably passed, practical French and British commanders saw that it would be a long time before independent American units could assume any appreciable portion of the combat burden. They began to insist almost immediately that American soldiers be fed into Allied divisions as replacements.

The Allies felt their request was logical. They had the experienced commanders and units, the necessary artillery, aviation, and tank support, but they lacked men. The American situation was the reverse. Their way, they argued, the power of the American soldier could be quickly brought to bear and hasten the victory. Yet this was reckoning without a sense of national pride that existed among both the soldiers themselves and the American people.

Pershing refused.

Although the Allied governments tried to bypass Pershing by going directly to Washington, they found the Secretary of War and the President firmly behind their field commander. When General Tasker H. Bliss, who had served briefly as the U.S. Army Chief of Staff, was sent as the American representative to the Supreme War Council, Allied governments tried this channel to break Pershing's adamant resolve; but although Bliss was inclined to be more conciliatory than Pershing, he yielded nothing on the principle of a separate American force.

The issue arose again early in 1918 when the British offered to provide the shipping to transport 150 battalions of infantry, which would be used to fill out British divisions that because of the manpower shortage had been reduced from 12 battalions of infantry to 9. After four or five months, according to the British plan, Pershing might withdraw the battalions to form them into American divisions.

This too Pershing refused, but well aware that a lack of ships was slowing the American build-up, he suggested that the British transport divisions instead. Because the same shipping that could move 150 infantry battalions could accommodate only about 3 divisions, which would mean only 36 infantry battalions, the British declined, but eventually they agreed to transport 6 divisions without equipment on the condition that Pershing outfit and train them in the British zone. Ten divisions would eventually arrive under this program.

The matter of a separate American force stood for the moment with Pershing still in unqualified control, yet in view of Allied persistence and of pending developments at the front the question was bound to arise again and again.

The German Offensive, March 1918

As the year 1918 opened, two more U.S. divisions were destined for early arrival in France, but if Pershing kept to his training schedule the American presence was a long way from assertion on the battlefield. The original excitement among the French and British over America's entry into the war had given way to renewed pessimism, for the Allied position appeared less favorable than at any time since the opening battle of the Marne. To the weary French and British, President Wilson's January proclamation of a 14-point peace proposal, however statesmanlike, appeared too idealistic.

So perturbed by the shocking losses of Passchendaele was the British Prime Minister, Lloyd George, that he withheld replacements to assure that his field commander, Sir Douglas Haig, would have to remain on the defensive. Nor could a French Army not yet fully recovered from the mutinies be expected to swing to the attack. The Allies appeared to have no alternative for 1918 but to hold on grimly until enough American troops arrived to assure the numerical superiority essential to victory.

Aside from the calamities of the Nivelle offensive, Passchendaele, and Caporetto, the Allies faced the prospect of sharply increased German numbers made available by the Russian defection. The number of German divisions shifted from east to west would have been even greater had the new Bolshevik government not reneged on its decision to get out

87

of the war and had the Germans not blundered in response. The Bolsheviks had come to Brest-Litovsk in December 1917 to talk only of a peace that would restore Russia's prewar boundaries and impose no indemnities, a concept that strained German credulity. What came of the first encounter at Brest-Litovsk was neither peace nor war but a bizarre new confrontation between Germany and Russia that still tied down eighty German divisions.

Russia, said the Bolsheviks, would not make peace; neither would its forces continue the war even if the Germans still fought. In response, the German armies in the east began in February 1918 to march deeper into Russia. They marched on even after the Bolsheviks at last agreed to real peace, only to become involved eventually in guerrilla warfare against their rear. Throughout the spring and summer of 1918 a million Germans that might have been decisive on the Western Front remained embroiled in Russia.

Within Germany, by the start of 1918, the duo of Hindenburg and Ludendorff had gradually accumulated almost dictatorial powers, with Ludendorff dominating more than ever. They decided that they had to strike early in 1918 in a final grand effort to achieve victory in the west before American manpower could be brought to bear. Germany, possibly more than France and Britain, was hurting gravely from the long war: on the home front, starvation was becoming a stark reality, and the previous summer there had been Marxist-inspired mutinies in the German Navy. The replacements going to German divisions were old men and boys.

By recalling divisions from Italy and some from the east, Ludendorff managed to assemble over 3,500,000 men on the Western Front, including 192 divisions. He planned to attack in early spring with 62 divisions along the Somme against the British, whose armies had little space for recoil before they would find themselves with their backs on the Channel. Having split the British and French, he then would turn to defeat the French. *(Map 4)*

For success Ludendorff counted on numerical superiority

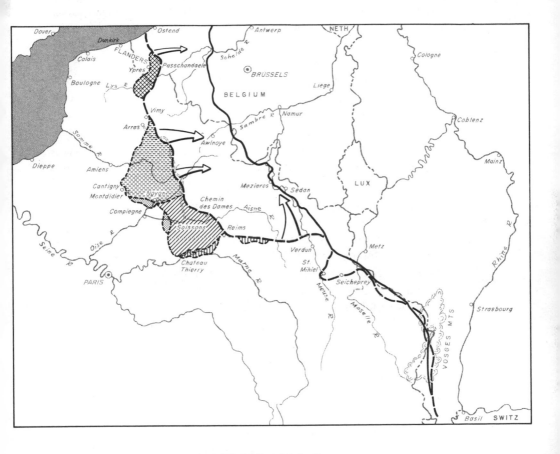

WESTERN FRONT

20 Mar – 11 Nov 1918

— · — · —	FRONT LINE, 20 MAR
	GERMAN AMIENS OFFENSIVE
	GERMAN LYS OFFENSIVE
	GERMAN AISNE OFFENSIVE
	GERMAN NOYON–MONTDIDIER OFFENSIVE
	GERMAN FINAL OFFENSIVE
⟶	ALLIED OFFENSIVE, SEP – NOV
——	FRONT LINE, 11 NOV

0   50

MILES

MAP 4

(4 to 1), surprise, and the first mass application of new tactics developed originally in the east by Lt. Gen. Oscar von Hutier. The so-called "Hutier tactics" involved a relatively short (several hours) but intensive artillery preparation, heavy on gas and smoke, followed by a rolling barrage creeping ahead of the infantry at a predetermined rate. Organized in small battle groups built around a light machine gun, the infantry infiltrated to cut off strongpoints rather than assault them, leaving that task to others who came behind. The enemy's forward positions ruptured, the infantry advanced swiftly to overrun the enemy artillery and break into the clear. In both these phases, light artillery was attached to assault battalions, a tactical use of horse-drawn field heretofore considered suicidal in trench warfare.

The new tactics put a premium on courage, stamina, initiative, and co-ordination, qualities which, for lack of time, the Germans could instill in only about two dozen specially selected divisions. These were pulled from the line, filled out with men from other divisions, and put through an intensive training program.

Despite elaborate efforts to achieve surprise, a new confidence radiating from Berlin and intelligence gathered from prisoners at the front made it clear to the Allies that the Germans were readying a major offensive. The British even determined the general strength, place, and finally the date of the attack, and they had a strong indication of the tactics the Germans would employ. But Haig, short of reserves, could do little in advance to prepare to counter the blow, while the French High Command refused to believe that if Ludendorff intended a decisive offensive he would strike the British rather than the French.

The big blow came on March 21 in a fog with the main effort against the British right wing. When night fell, the Germans had achieved a penetration along a 50-mile front and were pointing toward Amiens, a communications hub on the Somme that in German hands would effectively split the French and British armies. The only question remaining was, did Ludendorff have the means to exploit his success.

If Ludendorff's success or failure depended on early

90

commitment of Allied reserves, he had little cause for concern. Despite a mutual pledge by Haig and Pétain to go to each other's aid in event of crisis, so imbued was Pétain with the belief that the Germans were bound to strike a harder blow against the French that he was slow to send help. Although he gradually dispatched six divisions to the south flank of the penetration, these acted less to stem the German tide than to screen against any German turn toward Paris.

Ludendorff nevertheless was running into trouble. To broaden the penetration at the northern shoulder, he threw in 20 more divisions; but these were untrained in the Hutier tactics and failed to pierce a solid British defense. The long-fought-over terrain along the Somme slowed the advance of the main effort, and a hastily created British defensive force composed mainly of rear-echelon service troops occupied old trenches east of Amiens to halt the advance on that critical city. The German divisions in the lead were becoming exhausted, and supplies failed to get forward.

By the end of March, Ludendorff's offensive had bogged down. He had achieved a brilliant tactical victory—an advance of forty miles in eight days, 70,000 prisoners, 200,000 other Allied casualties; but strategically the result was empty. He had failed either to destroy the British armies or to separate them from the French, and he had taken as many casualties as he had inflicted, most of them in the highly trained shock divisions, losses he could not replace.

Unity of Command

A combination of the crisis and of Pétain's dilatory response to Haig's pleas for help also harmed German chances of ultimate victory. Although Haig himself had vitiated an earlier attempt to create a 30-division reserve for the Supreme War Council by pleading inability to spare his quota, he was so shaken by the crisis on the Somme that he volunteered to subordinate British troops around Amiens to a Frenchman, General (later Marshal of France) Ferdinand

Foch. As an instructor in prewar years at the École de Guerre, Foch had established a reputation as a military theorist and earlier in the war had successfully co-ordinated British, French, and Belgian operations in Flanders. Out of this agreement to subordinate all troops around the Amiens salient to Foch grew a broader understanding to subordinate, first, all British and French troops on the Western Front, then, later, all Allied forces.

The Allies at last had a unified command, even though they qualified it with weakening provisos: one that Foch had only "strategic direction" while "tactical control" remained with national commanders, another that each national commander could appeal a decision of the supreme commander to his home government. These qualifications, in theory, sharply diminished Foch's authority; but through military acumen, determination, and force of personality, Foch would make the arrangement work.

The Lys Offensive, April 1918

Ludendorff, meanwhile, clung to a belief that with another blow he could shatter the British armies. This time he chose a point a few miles north of the Amiens salient along the Lys River in Flanders, close by the scene of the bloody British offensive known as Passchendaele. Now he had 35 divisions.

Following an intensive bombardment, mainly with gas shells, eight German divisions attacked early on April 9 along the south bank of the Lys and quickly took advantage of the collapse of a Portuguese division to plunge five miles past the last of the trenches into open country. The next day other divisions attacking along the north bank of the Lys also achieved a penetration.

By the fourth day of the attack, the British were in serious danger. Putting the new unified command to a test, Field Marshal Haig called on Foch for help, but having long observed the tenacity of the British soldier on defense, Foch was convinced Haig could hold without involving reserves that could be better saved for a counteroffensive once the Germans had exhausted their resources. Although Haig fumed, Foch would agree to send only a few divisions.

Haig at that point issued what became known as his "backs to the wall" order: "There is no other course open to us but to fight it out. . . . With our backs to the wall and believing in the justice of our cause, each one of us must fight on to the end."

As the British soldier responded nobly, hungry German troops often slowed their attack to forage for food. In the end, Ludendorff had no choice but to call off the offensive. As April drew to a close, he held another vulnerable salient that included the Passchendaele Ridge but little else of tactical importance, this at a cost to the British of 305,000 casualties of all types but to the Germans even more, 350,000.

The first major action involving an American division had developed in the meantime far from the flaming Somme and Lys on a quiet sector in Lorraine, not far from the town of St. Mihiel. Here the 26th Division on April 20 came under a heavy bombardment, followed by a German attack in regimental strength aimed at seizing the village of Seicheprey. Boxing in the defenders with artillery barrages, the Germans took the village, only to lose it in the afternoon to a U.S. counterattack. The Germans held on to a nearby wood through the day, but American riflemen, cut off and scattered early in the fighting, regrouped to regain their positions the next day. The Germans left behind 160 dead, but they took 136 prisoners and inflicted 634 casualties.

During these weeks, General Pershing came under renewed pressure from the British and French to make up losses in Allied divisions with individual American replacements. While Pershing at the height of the crisis on the Somme had offered to place U.S. troops at Foch's disposal, he had been thinking only of the existing crisis while remaining faithful in the long run to the concept of an autonomous American army. Long and sometimes tempestuous were the arguments, voluminous the cables between Allied capitals, but in the end Pershing would go only so far as to agree that infantry and engineers of the divisions being transported in British shipping might be brought to France ahead of their artillery. Allied commanders, including Foch, finally endorsed the principle of forming as soon as possible an independent American force.

The Aisne Offensive, May 1918

As these arguments proceeded, the front was for a few weeks relatively quiet. It was a quiet before a storm, for Ludendorff was determined to persist in his struggle in Flanders to pin the British armies against the Channel.

To draw off Allied reserves from Flanders, Ludendorff decided on a diversionary attack against the Chemin des Dames, an elongated, commanding ridgeline northeast of Paris covering Soissons. Although this was the sector where Pétain had feared attack in March, with no attack forthcoming he had progressively thinned the defense. So imbued with the natural strength of the position was the local commander that he had neglected to erect a defense in depth, concentrating his men instead on the forward slope of the Chemin des Dames. In the face of heavy bombardment combined with the Hutier tactics, he was inviting disaster.

It was not long in coming. Although forewarned by an American intelligence analysis that an attack was in the offing, the French refused to heed the signs until the day before the attack was to begin. All the French troops could do in the time remaining was to stand warily at their posts while Foch belatedly began moving reserves.

With 17 divisions forward and 13 in follow-up reserve, the Germans attacked early on May 27 behind a barrage by close to 5,000 guns. German infantry plunged quickly over and beyond the Chemin des Dames, jumping the Aisne and Vesle Rivers, and gaining up to 20 miles in the first 24 hours.

Although this was to have been but a diversionary attack, Ludendorff was too elated by the breakthrough, too tempted by the open road to Paris to bring it to a halt. Three days later, on the last day of May, his troops would reach the Marne at Château-Thierry, less than fifty miles from the French capital, almost as close as Moltke had come in 1914.

Under pressure of this new crisis, General Pershing again went to Foch, this time to offer 5 American divisions to be used along the Marne as Foch deemed necessary. By the night of May 31, the machine gun battalion of the 3d Division, moved up swiftly in trucks, was in position to help French troops hold the bridge site over the Marne at Château-Thierry, and the rest of the division was on the way to help hold the river line. The next day the 2d Division (which included a Marine brigade) took up defensive positions north of the Marne and west of Château-Thierry astride the main highway to Paris.

Despair gripped not only the French stragglers falling back from the front but also the Allied High Command. What they could not know was that again Ludendorff was overextended, that he could strike in earnest for Paris only after broadening the wings of his narrow salient and bringing up supplies and reserves.

For two days Ludendorff's advance troops beat vainly against a hastily dug American line. At last they desisted, but the infantrymen and marines of the 2d Division would give them no rest. Beginning on June 6, the 2d Division attacked in costly but intrepid strikes against Belleau Wood and the villages of Bouresches and Vaux. Although this fighting would continue for three weeks, it was apparent from the first that the sudden, dramatic introduction of a new force had brought Ludendorff's thrust to a halt. For the Americans it was a costly debut—9,777 casualties, including 1,811 dead—but the moral effect on both sides was great.

The moral effect was all the more pronounced because of another action that antedated the 2d Division's achievement, the first offensive by an American division in the war. It began as a preliminary to a planned French counterattack against the Amiens salient, a counterattack that because of Ludendorff's breakthrough to the Marne failed to come off. It was an attack by the 1st Division against the village of

95

Cantigny on commanding ground near the tip of the salient.

Supported by American and French artillery and by French tanks, one regiment took the village in a swift maneuver early on May 28, then held on grimly as counterattack followed counterattack into the next day. The Americans lost 1,607 men, including 199 killed, but in the process they achieved a victory presaging greater events to follow.

The German Offensive, June 1918

Conscious of this new force entering the battle, conscious too of the necessity to maintain the initiative if ever the British armies were to be broken, Ludendorff wanted to pull back from the highly vulnerable Marne salient, but the effect on German morale would have been too adverse. Denied use of these troops for renewing the offensive against the British in Flanders, he decided on still another diversionary attack. By taking ground that might serve as a buffer for a railroad passing through Soissons, Ludendorff would improve supply into the Marne salient and at the same time pose a new threat to Paris that would, he hoped, pull Allied reserves from Flanders.

Ludendorff on June 9 sent one army westward from Soissons, another southward from the south flank of the Amiens salient between the towns of Noyan and Montdidier. As the two thrusts joined, they would merge the Amiens and Marne salients into one big, less vulnerable bulge in the line and release divisions to move to Flanders.

Yet this time there was no surprise and this time the French were ready with a defense in depth. They held the Germans to a tortuous advance of nine miles, then stopped them with counterattacks. By the fifth day, the attack had run its course.

A Growing American Force

As a temporary lull settled over the front, General Pershing on July 4 announced that a million Americans had arrived in France. Nine divisions had had some combat experience, mainly in quiet sectors; 2 others were completing their training; and 8 more had recently arrived. The total was 19, each one double the size of an Allied or German division.

In June Pershing had created three corps headquarters. The I Corps under Maj. Gen. Hunter Liggett first took responsibility for a sector near Château-Thierry, while the II Corps under Maj. Gen. George W. Read controlled the 27th and 30th Divisions that were destined to fight through the rest of the war with the British. The III Corps under Maj. Gen. Robert L. Bullard had yet to enter the line.

With 250,000 U.S. troops arriving very month, the effect of the American presence on Allied troops and the French population was stimulating, electric. Winston Churchill saw it this way:

> The impression made upon the hard-pressed French by this seemingly inexhaustible flood of gleaming youth in its first maturity of health and vigour was prodigious. None were under twenty, and few over thirty. As crammed in their lorries they clattered along the roads, singing the songs of a new world at the tops of their voices, burning to reach the bloody field, the French Headquarters were thrilled with the impulse of new life. . . . Half trained, half organized, with only their courage, their numbers and their magnificent youth behind their weapons, they were to buy their experience at a bitter price. But this they were quite ready to do.

For all the influx of new strength, no one yet saw any quick ending of the war, any indication that the Germans might have only one more offensive left in them.

97

The Last German Offensive, July 1918

The meager gains of Ludendorff's diversionary attack in June having failed either to secure the railroad at Soissons or to draw Allied reserves from Flanders, Ludendorff planned yet another diversionary attack before returning to the offensive in Flanders. A month in preparation, the new offensive began on July 15, one army driving southeast from the Marne salient, another attacking south from positions east of the city of Reims, a total of 52 divisions. Meeting on the Marine, the two armies were to cut a sizable segment from the Allied line and in the process solve the supply problem in the Marne salient by taking the railroads at Reims.

Ludendorff called this the *Friedensturm*—Peace Offensive. That was a mistake, for should failure occur in an offensive associated with such a grandiose aim, the German soldier would be in no condition to recover from the despair that was bound to follow. The slackening of discipline among troops too long denied all but the barest necessities had first emerged in the Lys offensive, but it had become even more apparent during the drive to the Marne as many men deserted the battle to loot wine cellars in the champagne country around Soissons. Weak from malnutrition, the soldiers were peculiarly susceptible to an influenze epidemic that swept the trenches in June and was to keep recurring into November. On the eve of each new offensive, hundreds were deserting to the enemy.

A wave of desertions combined with information gleaned from aerial photographs, observation posts, and patrols told the French what was coming, when, and where. East of Reims, the French commander, whose troops included the 42d U.S. Division, elected to pull the bulk of his men from the forward trenches, leaving only outposts in what was known as a "sacrifice line." While the vacated positions absorbed the German artillery bombardment, the French laid down a counterbarrage. As German troops battered by shellfire neared the "sacrifice line," French and American troops fell back to an intermediate position. After repeating

98

the delaying tactics, French and Americans again withdrew, this time to a main line of resistance. At this third line they held. By noon of the first day the issue was no longer in doubt.

Anxious to deny any German foothold across the Marne, the French opposite the other prong of the German attack had opted against these tactics. Here German gains were greater—up to four miles beyond the Marne at some points—and a French division, occupying a re-entrant formed by a bend in the river, folded, leaving four attached American companies of the 28th Division in a desperate plight. Most of these men were killed or captured. Yet the 3d Division on the French left held, its 38th Infantry, beset on three sides, executing such a steadfast defense that the regiment earned a nickname, "Rock of the Marne."

By noon of the second day, Ludendorff recognized that this prong of his attack also had been blunted. He called off the offensive.

Allied Counteroffensive

Even as the Germans were preparing what turned out to be their last offensive, General Foch had been assembling Allied divisions to launch a counteroffensive directed at first toward a limited objective—cutting the highway leading from Soissons to Château-Thierry, the main supply route of German troops in the Marne salient—but with the certainty that, if successful, the attack would be extended to erase the entire salient. In the forefront of the attack were two U.S. divisions—the 1st and 2d—operating under a French corps command.

A heavy rain fell as the troops moved to their jump-off positions the night of July 17, providential, as it turned out, since it helped conceal Allied preparations. After only a short but intensive artillery preparation early on the 18th, Allied infantry moved to the attack from near Soissons in the north to Château-Thierry in the south. In the corps with U.S. divisions, 350 French tanks early took the lead. When

MEN OF THE 26TH DIVISION NEAR CHÂTEAU-THIERRY, *July 1918.*

night fell, the two armies had advanced in some places up to five miles.

Although these two U.S. divisions were soon relieved by French and British units, the drive continued and expanded to the east, bringing in the 3d, 4th, 26th, and 28th Divisions and eventually the 32d, 42d, and 77th Divisions, and headquarters of the I and III Corps. The Germans began abandoning their Marne salient, though deliberately and in good order, retiring to successive defensive positions all the way to the Vesle River with the Chemin des Dames at their backs.

A Separate American Army

As the Allied drive came to a halt at the end of the first week of August, new hope of victory stirred in the ranks. The drive had carried no more than 20 miles, but the results were infinitely more important than the amount of territory regained. The counteroffensive had eliminated the threat to Paris, spoiled Ludendorff's cherished ambition of striking a deathblow in Flanders, and so dimmed German chances of victory that even Ludendorff could no longer hope for more than a stalemate. Furthermore, the initiative had passed to the Allies, whose fresh force had proven beyond doubt (though at a cost of 50,000 casualties) its ability on the offensive. In the bid to win before the Americans could intervene in force, Ludendorff had failed.

As this counteroffensive (sometimes called, in conjunction with the last German offensive, the Second Battle of the Marne) neared an end, General Pershing pressed his case for an independent American army and a separate sector of the front. Foch was sympathetic, for a separate American force fitted in with plans he was formulating to eliminate three other German-held salients on the front. British and French together were to reduce the Amiens salient, then the British would erase the Lys salient while the Americans eliminated another salient in Lorraine that had stood for

AMERICAN MILITARY POLICE PATROLLING A ROAD *near*
Château Thierry.

four years and took its name from a town at the tip, St. Mihiel.

With Pershing himself as commander, headquarters of the First Army officially opened on August 10. The new command encompassed the I and III Corps and 19 U.S. divisions.

As demonstrated earlier in making American units available to Allied armies, Pershing for all his adamant resolve to create an independent American force never objected to allowing some U.S. divisions to fight under Allied command; he objected instead to the use of American troops as individual replacements or in small increments to fill out depleted Allied units. Even as he formed the First Army he left the II Corps and its two divisions with the British, while he allowed several other divisions to serve under French command.

The one division whose employment violated Pershing's principle was the 93d, which had only infantry regiments without trains or artillery. This was a Negro division, one of only two organized and sent to France during the war, although thousands of other Negroes served overseas in the Services of Supply. The 93d's regiments were assigned to the French, reorganized according to French tables, and used as integral parts of French divisions. The other Negro division, the 92d, served in the First Army.

The Somme Offensive

As Pershing was forming the First Army, French and British armies under Haig launched converging attacks from the northwest and southwest against the Amiens salient. They achieved as much surprise as had the Germans against the Chemin des Dames. Using 300 tanks in the lead, ten British divisions, including Australians and Canadians, scored a swift breakthrough, brushing aside German units in rout, gaining seven miles in the first few hours, and making of August 8, in Ludendorff's words, a "black day" for the German Army.

Yet the slow, ponderous tanks could not long sustain such a pace, and horse cavalry was of no use when the enemy stiffened. Coming against a strong German stand in old trenches dating from 1915, Haig paused, shifted the emphasis of his attack farther north, then in a methodical campaign gradually pushed the Germans back. By the end of August the Germans were retiring into the positions whence they had begun their big March offensive, the Hindenburg Line. The Amiens salient, like that on the Marne, was a thing of the past. Meanwhile, other British units helped by the U.S. II Corps with the 27th and 30th Divisions had almost finished erasing the Lys salient.

On the German side, the events of 8 August had cast a pall over the High Command. "We have nearly reached the limit of our power to resist," said Hindenburg. "The war must be ended." When Ludendorff agreed, Wilhelm II instructed his Foreign Secretary to find a way out of the war, but the underlying idea was to retain as much as possible of the territory that the German armies had conquered. Under such a condition, there was little real hope for peace.

The St. Mihiel Offensive

As the British drive progressed, General Pershing and his staff shifted divisions to Lorraine. Their goal was to push beyond the St. Mihiel salient to seize Metz or at least to cut the highway running from Metz all the way to Antwerp, the enemy's main line of lateral communications. When Foch saw the plan, he was so enthusiastic that he increased the French participation from 4 to 10 divisions.

Foch's endorsement of the American plan preceded the British success in pushing the Germans into the Hindenburg Line. Planning an early attack along the Somme to break that line, Marshal Haig suggested to Foch that instead of attacking toward Metz the Americans should be employed from positions west of Verdun to attack northward toward Mézières along the French-Belgian frontier northeast of Reims. Such an attack would serve not only to cut the

104

FRENCH TANKS RETURNING FROM THE FRONT.

enemy's railroad but also to converge with the British attack.

Seeing in Haig's proposal a possibility of victory before the year was out, Foch endorsed the idea. Presenting it to General Pershing, he directed that once the St. Mihiel salient was eliminated the American objective should be changed from Metz to Mézières. In the drive On Mézières, Foch was to employ two armies, one wholly American under Pershing, the other Franco-American under French command.

Foch's proposal for a Franco-American army under French command appeared to Pershing as a threat to the long-sought independent American force which he had so recently achieved. He insisted that, while the American army "will fight wherever you may decide, it will not fight except as an independent American army." Foch declined to press the issue.

Reducing the scope of the attack on the St. Mihiel salient to nine U.S. and five French divisions, Pershing and his staff began to prepare two offensives to be mounted within 23 days in areas 40 miles apart. That was something no single army had yet attempted on the Western Front.

The Germans, fortunately, were to make the task easier. Conscious of the vulnerability of the St. Mihiel salient and of a major Allied offensive in the making, they began to pull out of the salient two days before Pershing planned to attack.

Under Pershing's plan, a French corps was to press the tip of the salient while the V Corps under Maj. Gen. George H. Cameron, in its first combat action, hit the west flank. Meanwhile General Liggett's I Corps and the IV Corps under Maj. Gen. Joseph T. Dickman, also new in the line, was to attack the south flank, the two American thrusts to meet in the center of the salient at the town of Vigneulles. French and British provided the bulk of the artillery support—3,000 guns—while the only tanks available were 267 light French Renaults. Although the French furnished many of the tank crews, others were Americans of the 304th Tank Brigade, commanded by Lt. Col. George S. Patton, Jr. An Allied air force controlled by an exponent of air power, Col. William Mitchell, consisted of almost 1,500 planes (600 piloted by Americans), the largest concentration of aircraft yet assembled.

Following a four-hour artillery bombardment, the tank-infantry advance began before daylight on September 12. Most of the tanks fell victim early to mechanical failure or mud, but they were hardly needed. Resistance was from the first surprisingly moderate, particularly on the southern flank where the Germans had already thinned their forward troops as a step in the general withdrawal. By nightfall of the first day a gap of only ten miles separated the two converging American forces.

When Pershing learned that roads leading out of the salient were filled with withdrawing Germans, he urged continued attack through the night to block all escape routes. A regiment of the 26th Division pushed swiftly from the west to enter Vigneulles two hours after midnight, there to be joined soon after dawn by a regiment of the 1st Division.

This first victory of the war by an American army netted 15,000 prisoners at a cost of only 7,000 casualties. It was so easy that some have referred to it as the action in which the Americans relieved the Germans, but the observation fails to take into account that the Germans had begun to pull back because they dreaded what was coming.

The Meuse-Argonne Offensive

Even as Pershing had been preparing and launching this first big American attack, Foch's original plan had been growing by bounds. No longer was the offensive to be confined to a British strike along the Somme and an American drive on Mézières. The new plan also included a Belgian-British-French attack along the Lys and French attacks in between British and Americans. It was to be a grand assault all along the front—said Foch: "Tout le monde à la bataille!" The aim was to cut the enemy's rail line at Mézières and Aulnoye, the latter in front of the British, and thereby force the Germans to retire inside their frontier before winter set in. For the offensive Foch had 220 divisions—160 in line, 60 in reserve. They included 42 of the big American divisions, although some of these had only recently arrived and Pershing would be forced to cannibalize others to obtain replacements. Ten American divisions would still serve with British and French armies.

Assisted by the French Fourth Army on the left, the American attack was to begin first, on September 26. It posed a tremendous logistical effort involving rapid transfer of some 800,000 men, 200,000 French moving out of the new American sector west of Verdun, and 600,000 Americans moving in. That it was completed in secrecy and in time for the jump-off was attributable in large measure to the planning of a young officer on Pershing's staff, Col. George C. Marshall. Again the British and French furnished most of the artillery and tanks (190 French lights) and some of the 800 aircraft supporting the attack.

The terrain over which the advance was to pass was studded with natural and man-made obstacles. From high ground east of the Meuse River, which formed the right boundary for the attack, and from densely wooded high ground of the Argonne Forest in the left of the attack zone, German eyes could look down on much of the battlefield; and in the center, between the forest and the river, the Germans held a hogback ridge replete with fortified spurs and stone-walled villages. The Germans had established three lines with trenches, barbed wire, deep dugouts, and concrete fighting posts, while a fourth was under construction farther back. Particularly formidable were strongpoints at Montfaucon, Cunel, and Barricourt.

In a sector approximately twenty miles wide, Pershing massed three corps, each to employ two divisions forward, one in reserve. With a superiority in men of 8 to 1, he hoped to make the ten miles through the first three German positions in one sustained drive.

The infantry began to advance before daylight after a 3-hour artillery bombardment. Achieving surprise, they caught the Germans with only four divisions in the line. General Bullard's III Corps on the right pushed five miles through both the first and second German positions, but

General Cameron's V Corps in the center ground to a halt before the bristling defenses of Montfaucon, and General Liggett's I Corps on the left could advance little more than a mile through the thick, almost trackless Argonne Forest.

During the next few days, the troops plodded slowly forward, at last carrying Montfaucon and putting the V Corps through the second German line, but progress amid the trees and dank ravines of the Argonne Forest still was slow. Flanking fire from east of the Meuse and from uncleared portions of the Argonne harried units on the right and in the center. Most of the supporting tanks succumbed to the usual troubles of mud and mechanical failure. Congestion and muddy roads hampered resupply. Most serious of all was the inexperience of the troops, for having used his experienced divisions in the St. Mihiel salient Pershing had had to withhold them from the first assault. Units got lost, message traffic broke down, some commanders failed.

Any hope that an advance by the French Army on the left might unhinge the Germans in front of the U.S. troops went for naught, for the French were making no more rapid gains. As September came to an end, Pershing had no choice but to pause to reorganize.

Elsewhere on the Western Front, progress was, with one exception, not much more encouraging. The Belgian-French-British effort on the Lys bogged down in rain and mud, as had every offensive in that region, while the French in the center of the Allied line were not to begin their attack until British and Americans on their flanks had driven deep enough to threaten the Germans opposite them with entrapment. Only the British along the Somme provided any indication of decisive success, scoring a deep penetration of the Hindenburg Line with the help of the 27th and 30th Divisions of the U.S. II Corps. The penetration was soon expanded to create a gap all the way through the fortifications, but the effort left British troops temporarily spent.

Despite the disappointing progress of the grand offensive from an Allied viewpoint, it was enough to start a collapse within the German High Command. On September 28, Ludendorff mused at such length on the miseries besetting him that he worked himself into a rage, foamed at the mouth, and fell to the floor. That evening he called on Hindenburg. The situation, the two agreed, was infinitely worse than in August when they had first urged the kaiser to seek peace, advice that had produced no results. They had no alternative now but to agree to surrender all conquered territory in the west and try to negotiate a peace on the basis of President Wilson's Fourteen Points.

On October 4 the German chancellor cabled Wilson asking for an armistice. Without informing the Allied governments, Wilson answered with a request for clarification. The German chancellor replied on October 12 that the Germans agreed to all Fourteen Points; but by this time word of the peace feeler had reached the French and British, who for their part were in no mood to accept Wilson's unilateral actions. Furthermore, Ludendorff himself had recovered from his convulsive fit, had seen that the Allied offensive had imposed no rout, and had come to believe the Germans could get terms that would allow them to withdraw behind their own frontier, reorganize their armies, and resist any peace proposals they deemed unacceptable.

Yet events were taking place that were destined to tie Ludendorff's hands and harden Wilson's resolve. Not the least of these were continued fierce German resistance and the revelation, in those areas where the Germans were forced to retire, of wanton destruction and a barbaric disregard for human life more flagrant than those excesses of 1917 when they had left behind a wasteland in retiring into the Hindenburg Line.

On the Meuse-Argonne front, Pershing's First Army renewed its offensive on October 4 after inserting experienced divisions into the line, but during the brief pause in operations Ludendorff had brought in reinforcements. The fight to clear the rest of the Argonne Forest and pierce the third German line progressed no more swiftly than before.

In the Argonne a "lost battalion" of the 77th Division was surrounded for five days before other troops could break through to free 194 survivors out of an original 600. In the Agonne, too, an American patrol took about 75 Germans by

110

surprise and was herding them toward the rear when German machine gunners opened fire, killing and wounding 9 out of 17 in the patrol. When a German lieutenant led a charge aimed at the survivors, Pfc. Alvin C. York, a Tennessee sharpshooter, cut down 15 Germans one by one until at last surviving members of this group too surrendered. When a count could be taken, it revealed that York had captured 132 of the enemy.

To dispense with the troublesome German flanking fire from heights on the other side of the Meuse, General Pershing broadened his attack to include the east bank. To control that phase, Pershing created the Second Army under General Bullard. Relinquishing command of the First Army to General Liggett, Pershing himself moved up to the level of army group.

Despite the added strength on the east bank, the fight continued slow and costly, for Ludendorff looked on the offensive as such a threat to the vital railroad through Mézières that he eventually committed 27 of his reserve divisions to this sector. Some help developed on the left when on October 5 the U.S. 2d Division, attacking with the French, captured high ground known as Blanc Mont, prompting a slow German withdrawal before the Fourth Army back to the Aisne River. On the 10th, the I Corps finally cleared the last of the Argonne Forest, but bitter fighting continued through the rest of the month for the fortified hills between the forest and the Meuse. Not until the last day of October was the third German position broken all along the line.

The British in the meantime had renewed their offensive, driving forward inexorably as the Germans fell back grudgingly from one prepared position to another. It was in this section that much of the evidence of German destruction and barbarity was found.

At the same time, continuing activities of the U-boats also helped to crystallize Allied resolve. On the 10th, a submarine torpedoed a passenger steamer off the coast of Ireland with a loss of 300 lives. A few days later another U-boat sank an Irish mail boat taking the lives of 520 passengers, mostly women and children.

Affected by the public outcry over these incidents, President Wilson made clear in his reply to the second German note that the Allied military leaders would set the terms of the armistice, that there was no other way to deal with a government that persisted in illegal and inhumane acts. The note concluded that if the United States had to deal "with the military masters and the monarchial autocrats of Germany now, or if it is likely to have to deal with them later in regard to the international obligations of the German Empire, it must demand, not peace negotiations but surrender."

Confidence restored, Ludendorff called on his government to reject the terms; but the government was by this time listening to the voices of a disillusioned people, the noise of riots in the streets, and to the threat of Marxist revolution. On October 27 the kaiser dismissed Ludendorff, who repaired in disguise to Sweden, and events strode swiftly toward a climax. The German naval commander tried to take the High Seas Fleet to sea in a last bid for glory, but the crews mutinied and brought the ships back into port with revolutionary flags flying. Revolutionary councils formed among the soldiers in the trenches. Bulgaria in late September had already dropped out of the war; Turkey followed on October 30; Austria-Hungary on November 3. On November 6 Ludendorff's successor, General Wilhelm Groener, urged the government to conclude an armistice within three days or face chaos.

All along the front, meanwhile, the Allied armies had renewed their offensives in what became a general advance. In the far north two U.S. divisions—the 37th and 91st—fought with the Belgian-French-British force under the Belgian king. Haig's British troops entered their objective of Aulnoye on November 5, while the French armies maintained steady pressure against the German center.

Beginning on the first of November, the U.S. First Army renewed the attack with the V Corps in the center driving six miles the first day to take heights just south of the fourth German line near Barricourt. This feat assured success of the whole operation, for it prompted German withdrawal behind the Meuse. On November 5 the III Corps forced a crossing of the Meuse, and three days later American troops held high ground overlooking the city of Sedan, a few miles east of Mézières, and brought the lateral railroad under artillery fire. There the advance stopped as Marshal Foch shifted the American boundry eastward to allow the French the honor of retaking Sedan, scene of a disastrous French defeat in 1870.

The Meuse-Argonne was the greatest battle yet fought by the U.S. Army. Almost 1,250,000 American troops had participated during the course of the offensive. Casualties were high—120,000 of all types—but the results impressive. Until the last, this battle had worried German commanders most; unlike other sectors of the front, here they had little space short of a vital objective that they could afford to trade for time.

The German Surrender

Under pressure of continuing Allied attack and of public agitation at home, the Germans early on November 8 sent delegates to a railroad siding in the Compiègne Forest west of Soissons to discuss armistice terms. The next day the kaiser abdicated, fleeing to the Netherlands in exile, and the Germans proclaimed a republic.

Under terms of the armistice, the Germans were to withdraw from all occupied territory, including Alsace and Lorraine; retire all armies to the east bank of the Rhine; provide the Allies with bridgeheads beyond the Rhine; and relinquish specific amounts of military equipment that would preclude their continuing the war.

The fighting ended at the eleventh hour of the eleventh day of the eleventh month, 1918.

Men died right up to the last, but finally, after more than four grim years, it was over. Of the men of all nations in uniform, more than 8,500,000 died, and total casualties exceeded 37,500,000, a price that would forever invite criticism of the way commanders on both sides fought the war. American casualties alone totaled 320,710.

113

So ended the first adventure of the United States in departing from its traditional policy of noninvolvement in European affairs. That the nation could make such a decisive contribution in so short a time hardly could have been conceived in advance.

That there would be mistakes, blunders, shortcomings under such a rapid expansion and commitment was perhaps inevitable. Until mid-1918, for example, when separate replacement training camps were at last established, units both in the United States and overseas had to be broken up to provide replacements. This practice was damaging to morale and damaging too in that it sent many poorly trained men into the lines. So close did the American supply system in France come to breaking down that in the summer of 1918, under threat of intervention from Washington, Pershing had to exert special efforts to rescue it. Pershing himself was overburdened with command responsibilities—theater, line of communications, and tactical. The dependence on the Allies for air, artillery, and tank support, however inevitable in such a rapid deployment, did nothing for efficiency on the battlefield. On the home front some Americans vented their hostility on other Americans for no more valid reason than their ancestry.

Yet countless other things were done effectively. The nation handled conscription with minimum friction and without disruption of the economy. The Army expanded with almost incredible speed while still maintaining efficiency. The Navy performed invaluable service in defeating the submarine and, with British help, in getting the Army safely overseas. Although the war ended before American industry could demonstrate its full wartime potential, the record, with some exceptions, was impressive nevertheless.

Most important of all, the nation and its Army had provided a force that reached embattled Europe in time to rejuvenate flagging Allied fortunes and provide sufficient advantage to assure victory for the Allied side.

Index

119